# Streiker The Killdeer

## ROBIN HARDY

**NAVPRESS**

BRINGING TRUTH TO LIFE
NavPress Publishing Group
P.O. Box 35001, Colorado Springs, Colorado 80935

The Navigators is an international Christian orga-
nization. Jesus Christ gave His followers the Great
Commission to go and make disciples (Matthew
28:19). The aim of The Navigators is to help fulfill
that commission by multiplying laborers for
Christ in every nation.

NavPress is the publishing ministry of The
Navigators. NavPress publications are tools to help
Christians grow. Although publications alone cannot make disciples or change lives, they can help
believers learn biblical discipleship, and apply
what they learn to their lives and ministries.

© 1993 by Robin Hardy
All rights reserved. No part of this publication may
be reproduced in any form without written
permission from NavPress, P.O. Box 35001,
Colorado Springs, CO 80935.
Library of Congress Catalog Card Number:
93-37393
ISBN 08910-97635

Cover illustration: Bill Farnsworth

*Jesus Loves Me*, words by Anna B. Warner, 1860.

Hardy, Robin, 1955–
    Streiker the killdeer  /  Robin Hardy.
        p.    cm.
    Sequel to: Streiker's bride.
    ISBN 0-89109-763-5
    1. Eccentrics and eccentricities—United States—
Fiction. 2. Millionaires—United States—Fiction.
3. Marriage—United States—Fiction.  I. Title.
PS3558.A62387S82    1993
813¢.54—dc20                        93-37393
                                    CIP

Printed in the United States of America

*To my friend and editor*
*Steve Webb*
*who would rather be golfing*

# Prologue

Fletcher Streiker is a billionaire philanthropist who makes his home in Dallas, Texas. He is so reclusive that, in spite of great media interest, no one seems to know what he looks like and few people have seen him face to face.

*Streiker's Bride* tells of the unusual courtship and marriage of this man to Adair Weiss, who worked as a teller in a bank that he owned. Summoned to the office of Charles Whinnet, the bank president, Adair is handed a folder full of information about Streiker and told that he desires to meet her. However, since he values his privacy, they would not date in the customary manner. She would meet him in person only when she agreed to marry him.

After some intense struggling with his terms, Adair decides to accept his offer. Once they become husband and wife, she is overjoyed to find him to be all she could ever hope for. But the honeymoon is short-lived as he leaves on another business trip without even telling her where he is going. He tells her only that he will return shortly. Meanwhile, Adair is left to cope with new struggles and dangers as the wife of a powerful man with many enemies.

First, Adair must make the decision to trust him; then she must decide to carry out the assignments he leaves for her—tasks she finds humbling and sometimes incomprehensible. Moreover, an old friend turned enemy, Darren Loggia, begins to stalk her.

As Adair becomes increasingly anxious for Fletcher to return, Darren becomes increasingly bold, to the point of attacking her in her own apartment. But when Fletcher telephones the apartment and talks to him, Darren mysteriously leaves. Then Adair becomes convinced that she will see her husband at a party hosted by the Whinnets that evening.

At the party, she is bemused to see many people she knows. But Darren crashes the party as well to terrorize the guests. At this point Fletcher arrives, and when Darren attempts to shoot him, the gun explodes in Darren's hand, killing him. Fletcher takes Adair away in his private helicopter, and here we resume the story.*

---

* Please refer to the Glossary on pages 247-248 for definitions of Hawaiian terms.

❧

*For this cause shall a man leave his father and mother,*
*and shall be joined unto his wife,*
*and they two shall be one flesh.*
*This is a great mystery:*
*but I speak concerning Christ and the church.*
EPHESIANS 5:31-32

❧

*The Streiker books are intended to present an analogy*
*of Christ and the church, based on Ephesians 5:31-32.*
*As such, the stories and characters are fictitious,*
*and any resemblance to other individuals is coincidental.*

# 1

I n the darkness, he bent to her ear and whispered, "You have to."

Adair reached up to her new husband's face, visible only in outline. The *National Inquisitor* had offered $250,000 for a photograph of this face, and though she could not see it now, she carried it in her imagination: black hair, brown eyes, a splendid blending of his father's Anglo strength and his mother's Hawaiian tenderness. "I'm scared," she whispered back.

"What will they do, say no?" he chided softly, brushing back a tangle of her blond hair. "I'm right here," he added, standing close beside her at the pay phone.

"I'm not afraid they'll say no," she moaned, turning to the phone. "I'm afraid they'll say, 'Come right over.' Do you have that number?" She squinted at the piece of paper he held up as she dialed.

"Hello?" On recognizing her mother's slightly twangy voice, Adair nervously twisted the stiff phone cord. She had not heard this voice for about seven years now.

"Hello, Mom. This is Adair," she said carefully.

"Adair! Is it really you? Dale!" She turned to scream at Adair's stepfather, who was possibly in another room— or across town, judging from the volume. "*Dale!* Adair's on the line! Where are you, sweetheart?" she asked Adair.

"Well, Fletcher and I just flew in, and he. . . . I would like to bring him by to meet you, if it's not too late," Adair said without enthusiasm.

"Come right over!" her mother exclaimed. "Dale! Adair is bringing her *husband!*" *The billionaire!* is what Adair's mother communicated loud and clear. She had seen the newspaper accounts of the reclusive philanthropist's surprise marriage to her daughter.

Adair winced. "Mom, *please* don't tell *anybody* we're here. Fletcher has to . . . avoid publicity in order to continue his work. No photos, or. . . ."

"You mean I can't call your Aunt Becky and Uncle Pete?" Adair's mother asked, pained.

"Not yet, Mom, please," Adair pleaded. "It would create real problems for Fletcher."

"Well, all right," she reluctantly agreed. "Do you know where we live?"

Adair glanced up as Fletcher nodded. "Yes, Fletcher does. See you in a few minutes, Mom."

"Wonderful!" her mother exclaimed, as Adair hung up.

"She was real excited," Adair said dully.

"There now," Fletcher said. "Told you it wouldn't be so bad."

"We're not there yet," Adair muttered under her breath as Fletcher put in a quarter and dialed a number from memory.

He waited a moment, then said, "We're on our way to the Threadgills'," and hung up. With no hope of putting it off any further, Adair climbed into the waiting cab with Fletcher.

Around 9:30 p.m., the cab pulled up to a nice ranch-style home on a tidy Longview street. Emerging from the taxi, Fletcher handed the driver a folded bill. The driver looked at it and startled. "You want me to wait?"

"Why don't you come back in about an hour?" Fletcher suggested as he lent Adair a hand.

"You can count on it, guy." The cabbie saluted with two fingers and took off. Adair did not realize until much later that he never returned.

Fletcher walked Adair up to the lighted porch and rang the doorbell. She leaned into his side for his support. An instant later the door opened, and they looked down at a blond eight-year-old boy.

"Brian?" Adair said, and he nodded. The last time she had seen her half brother, he was just a baby. "I'm Adair, and this is my husband, Fletcher Streiker."

Fletcher stuck out his hand to Brian, who shook it and asked, "Will you buy me a remote-control car without any wires?"

"Sure," said Fletcher.

Brian turned, bumping into his mother, who had come up behind him. "Adair!" She reached out to hug her daughter, dragging her over the threshold in the process. Fletcher stepped inside and shut the door behind him. Brian ran off to summon his father.

"You must be Fletcher," Adair's mother said, reaching out a dainty hand. She shared Adair's high cheekbones, neon blue eyes, and a similar shade of frosted blond hair.

"Mrs. Threadgill," Fletcher said, shaking her hand.

"Call me Dana. I just can't believe this. Come sit down, you two. Something to eat? A nightcap?" She steered them to a comfortably furnished front room.

"No, thank you," Fletcher said, then turned as Brian ran in preceding his father—a large man, grown heavier since Adair had last seen him, with a canny, distrustful air and deliberately rumpled appearance. Without waiting for an introduction, Fletcher extended his hand. "Mr. Threadgill. Fletcher Streiker."

"Dale," he replied as he gripped Fletcher's hand. "So. . . ."

"Dad, he's going to buy me a remote-control car without any wires!" Brian eagerly shared.

Flustered, Dana scolded, "Brian, I warned you not to ask for anything." Turning to Fletcher, "Do sit down. Are you sure you wouldn't care for anything? I just put on a pot of coffee."

"I take mine black, thank you," Fletcher said, sitting with Adair on the velour sofa. Brian sat on the floor next to Fletcher's knees and Dale settled down on the love seat. Dana bustled out to get coffee. Sitting close beside Fletcher, Adair self-consciously tugged on the hem of her dress. She had been so hurried changing into this dress that she had not remembered it to be this short. The length of her skirts had precipitated many a fight with Dale.

There was an awkward silence as Dale regarded Fletcher and Fletcher smiled at Brian. Adair saw her high school senior portrait sitting on an end table and a ten-year-old dance picture hanging on the wall. From the condition of the frames, she guessed that they had been residing in a drawer until very recently. "So," Dale said, and Fletcher looked up, "what do you do for a living?"

"Well," Fletcher began slowly, "I spend a lot of time managing my company. Too much time. I'd like to pare that down."

"And what does this company of yours do?" Dale asked.

"Mostly, it manages my investments," Fletcher said, accepting his coffee from Dana with a quick smile.

·"Doesn't it *make* anything?" Dale asked in a tone of slight exasperation.

"I believe we do have several manufacturing concerns," Fletcher said, as if probing his memory.

"All this business talk is boring," Dana announced, sitting across from Fletcher. "You're much younger than I thought," she observed, and Fletcher raised his eyes over his coffee cup. "So, I'm dying to know how you met Adair."

"She worked in a bank I own," Fletcher replied.

"You worked in a bank?" Dana asked her daughter in astonishment. "How did you manage that? Your math grades were never very good."

Adair barely shrugged in reply, so Fletcher said, "She was pedaling pretty hard to make up for the math. She was taking accounting at night."

Dale snorted, "I told you that dance stuff was a waste of time."

Fletcher glanced at Adair, but again she said nothing, so he replied, "She'll have the opportunity to pursue that now, if she wants."

"Dance? Professionally?" Dana laughed. "Sweetheart, you can't; you're too old."

Adair looked at the wall. Fletcher waited a few seconds before opening his mouth. "At twenty-four?" he wondered.

"Oh yes," Dana said assuredly. "A dancer's life span is so short, no troupe will even consider somebody new who's out of her teens. Unless—oh, goodness, I'm forgetting. You could set her up in just about anything she wanted, couldn't you? All it would take would be one phone call from you, and she'd be dancing the lead in *Swan Lake*, wouldn't she?"

Adair did not say a word, but Brian suddenly scrambled to his feet and left the room. "What kind of investments did you say you had?" Dale asked.

Fletcher cleared his throat. "Well, there's some oil and gas, some real estate, and a lot of small business ventures. I like to finance people with offbeat ideas. That's kind of how I got my start."

Brian then returned to the room with a slender catalog. "That's the one I want," he said, pointing to a slick picture of a remote-control car.

"Brian!" Dana said in exasperation.

Fletcher took the catalog and dog-eared the page. "Can I take this?" he asked Brian.

"Sure!" the boy said. So Fletcher folded up the catalog and stuffed it in his jacket pocket. Adair smiled at him and Brian resumed his position in perfect satisfaction beside Fletcher's knees.

The atmosphere in the room changed somewhat as Brian's parents regarded Fletcher's responsiveness to him. Dana suddenly blushed. "Oh, look at that. I sat you right down on that tacky old couch with the loose spring. I'm so ashamed."

"I'm comfortable," Fletcher assured her.

"There's not a thing wrong with that couch," Dale returned a tad defensively. "You wanna talk tacky, you go look at that junk heap I drive to work every day."

"It's a heap, all right, but that's what you wanted," Dana countered. "*I* suggested a nice Cadillac, but *you* had to have the pickup. Now with all that we've spent on that crate, we can't afford a nicer car."

Dale was torn between defending himself and advancing his cause. "It's done okay, but it's gettin' ragged."

"Ragged! Look at the carpet under your feet for ragged! Do you realize we haven't replaced *any* carpet since we moved here?" Dana demanded.

"Why should we replace the carpet when the roof leaks all over it?" Dale's voice rose.

In the middle of Dana's stormy reply, Fletcher asked, "Is there something you'd like me to buy for you?"

They broke off their argument to stare at him. Then Dana blushed. "We're not much better than Brian, are we? I guess we hardly know how to handle a wealthy son-in-law."

"Just tell me what you want," Fletcher said. They looked at him, scarcely knowing how to respond. "Let's make this easy on everyone," he then suggested. "List it out. Make a list of what you want."

"Why don't you just write out a nice-sized check?" Dale countered, half in jest.

"I don't carry a checkbook, only traveling cash. All checks are written through the corporation," Fletcher replied.

Dana gestured uneasily. "Never mind that. We just want to get to know you."

"Now, Dana, you should take the man at his word. He says list it out, we list it out. Go get one of them pads—not the phone pad, a legal pad from the desk there," Dale instructed.

Hesitantly, Dana got up and retrieved a yellow pad and pen from the next room. While she sat beside Dale on the love seat to ponder their list, Brian asked Fletcher, "Where do you live?"

"Dallas," said Fletcher, turning toward him.

"How'd you get here?" Brian asked.

"We came partway in my helicopter, and the rest of the way in a cab," Fletcher said.

"A helicopter! Wow! Can I ride it sometime?" Brian asked eagerly.

"Yes. We'll have to get you to a place where I can

pick you up," said Fletcher.

"A pickup, first," mused Dale, writing. "A new Silverado."

"We *need* a family car first," Dana objected quietly.

"You pick me up? Can you fly a chopper?" Brian asked in amazement.

"Yes. My dad was a Navy pilot," Fletcher replied.

"No lie?" exclaimed Brian. "Did he teach you to fly?"

"He taught me just about everything worthwhile I ever learned," Fletcher said warmly.

"Well, put down your Cadillac as number two," Dale offered. "Number three: a boat. A thirty-four-foot sedan bridge Searay, loaded, with twin four-fifty-fours," Dale dictated to himself.

"Fully furnished," Dana interjected.

"That's what *loaded* means, dear," Dale said disparagingly.

"Did he ever take you fishing?" Brian asked wistfully.

"He took me everywhere with him, wherever he could take me. Mom got to calling me his little tick. He taught me how to treat people, and without knowing that I never would have been much of a success," Fletcher said.

"New carpet throughout the house," Dana said firmly.

"Heck, why not a new house?" Dale cracked, writing busily.

Brian glanced at his father and then down at the floor. "You don't have to get me that remote-control car," he said dully.

"I'd be happy to get you the car, Brian," Fletcher replied.

Brian looked up at him, then at Adair sitting quietly beside him. "What made you marry my sister?"

Fletcher eyed Adair, smiling. "Because I love her."

"But why?" Brian pressed.

"Because . . . she risked trusting me," Fletcher said. Brian made a puzzled face and Fletcher added, "Just take my word for it that it took a lot of guts for her to marry me. Besides . . ." He glanced at Adair and then leaned down to whisper something to Brian.

Snickering, the boy looked at his sister and admitted, "I guess so." Adair cocked a brow at Fletcher. "Do you have a boy?" Brian asked suddenly.

Fletcher paused before answering. Dana looked up and said, "Now, Brian, they haven't been married long enough to have any children. And. . . . you haven't been married before, have you?" she asked Fletcher uncertainly.

"No, I've never been married before," he said. Dana nodded in approval.

Dale held up the list for his wife's appraisal. "What're we missing, honey?"

She glanced at the paper. "It would be nice to have a new wardrobe," Dana confessed to Fletcher.

"Write it down," he said.

"What, is he going to send you a bunch of dresses from Dallas? Let's just say, oh, fifty thousand for incidentals," Dale proposed.

Dana looked inquiringly to Fletcher. "Put it on the list," he repeated.

Dale did, and Dana said, "I really think that's enough, Dale; don't you?"

He looked down the list of fourteen items. "Yeah, I guess so. Don't want our son-in-law to think we're trying to gouge him, do we?" Dale laughed. He carefully tore the sheet from the pad and extended it to Fletcher.

"My assistant will be handling this, so put your

name, address, and phone number on it," Fletcher instructed. "And both of you need to sign it." They did, and handed it over to him. He folded it and put it in his jacket pocket with Brian's catalog.

The doorbell rang. Adair looked in alarm at her mother, who pointedly stated, "I wonder who that could be?" as she got up to answer it. Dale suddenly looked uneasy.

Fletcher stood. "I think I'll have another cup of coffee. Adair? Dale?"

Adair shook her head and Dale said stiffly, "None for me, thanks," so Fletcher took his cup to the kitchen.

Just then a woman abruptly entered the front room with the flash of a pocket camera, taking hasty, random pictures. Dana was on her heels, exclaiming, "Patty! Stop that! Get out! Dale!"

He quickly rose from the love seat as Patty looked at Adair and Brian in disappointment. "Where's the billionaire?"

Dale took her arm and mumbled something to her as he escorted her back to the door. The bell rang again, and Brian jumped up to look out the front window. "Wow! Look at all the people in our front yard!"

Adair turned accusingly to her mother, who had hung back in some trepidation as Dale stood at the front door ordering gawkers home. Dana caught Adair's eye and insisted, "I did not tell anyone that you and Fletcher were coming over!"

"Look, Mom!" Brian said from the window. Dana went over to peek through the curtains, then closed them tightly and drew her son away.

As Dale returned to the room, Dana spun on him and demanded, "Dale Earl Threadgill, how did all those people know that Fletcher was here?"

He looked manifestly guilty. "Uh, I just called Ralph—

that's all, I swear. I had to call him, 'cause he's my best buddy down at the plant, and he *swore* he wouldn't tell a soul, that bald-faced liar."

Everyone turned to look at Fletcher, who had entered the room calmly sipping his coffee. He surveyed their faces, then remarked, "Looks like we'll have to stay here for a while, Dana."

Adair sagged mutely. She had not so much as a toothbrush with her. Dana became flustered at the prospect of enduring some inconvenience on account of her guests and cringed as the doorbell rang again. "Good heavens . . . I haven't got a thing to eat in the house. . . . The guest bedroom's a mess. . . ."

"It won't be for long," Fletcher assured her. As Adair listened to all this, anger at her mother and her step-father almost drew tears to her eyes.

"Neat! You can sleep in my room with me!" Brian exclaimed.

Fletcher laughed. "You're a great kid, but I'd rather sleep with my wife. Dana, please show us where."

With an inadvertent look of irritation, Dana took them down the hall and opened the door to a spare bedroom. It was cluttered with storage items and craft supplies. As Dana began taking cushions off the sofa sleeper, she told her daughter, "Get sheets and pillows from the linen closet."

Adair went down the hall, opening doors until she came to the closet. She brought back bedding, which she placed on a chair while Fletcher and her mother unfolded the bed. "Dana! Telephone!" Dale called from the other room.

Dana threw up her hands and excused herself with "Let me know if you need anything else" on her way out of the room.

Fletcher closed the door behind her. Adair began

placing sheets on the sleeper mattress while trying not to cry. Fletcher came up behind her and slipped his arms around her waist. She closed her eyes and inhaled, leaning back against him. "It's every bit the disaster I knew it would be," she whispered.

He laughed. "Adair, you've got to start using what you know about people. Accept your parents for who they are and don't sweat it."

She turned in his arms. "You're not really going to buy them all that stuff, are you?"

"Sure. Why not?" he asked.

"Because then they'll just demand more and more and more!" she hissed.

"That's one hypothesis," he said amiably. "Don't worry about them. Use that energy for something else." He kissed her and Adair laced her arms around his neck. Then they lay down on the skimpy, lumpy mattress.

"I missed you," he said into her neck as Adair began unbuttoning her dress. She paused at a soft knock on the door.

Fletcher got up and opened the door. Outside stood Brian, fidgeting in his pajamas. "I'm supposed to be in bed," he whispered, casting a guilty glance down the hall, "but I wanted to ask you a question."

Fletcher gestured for him to come in, then shut the door behind him. "What is it?"

"I wanted to come ask you—you're going to say no," Brian despondently forecast.

"Maybe," said Fletcher. "But we won't know till you ask, will we?"

"Yeah," grumbled Brian. "What it was, was. . . . I wanted to know if I could come live with you. I want to come live with you."

Adair quickly looked to Fletcher for his reaction. With a perfectly straight face, he said, "No you don't.

You're just saying that."

"I'm not either," protested Brian. "I really do. I really want to."

"I don't believe it. You're joshing me," Fletcher repeated.

"I'm not either! I mean it!" Brian said earnestly.

"Prove it," Fletcher dared him.

"How?" Brian asked.

Fletcher turned to a cluttered table behind him for a pen and scrap of paper. "Here's my address in Dallas," he said, writing. "The Streiker Corporation. If you really mean what you say, then you write to me. Each time you write me, I'll write you back. If you keep in touch with me, then when I see you mean business, I'll come get you."

"In your chopper?" Brian asked excitedly.

"Yes," replied Fletcher.

"When?" Brian asked, clutching the paper.

"When I see that it's time," said Fletcher.

"But how long?" whined Brian, and in his question Adair heard echoes of her repeated query, *How long will you be gone?*

"I don't know. That's up to you. When you've convinced me you mean it, I'll come," Fletcher said airily.

Brian's bright blue eyes narrowed in suspicion. "How do I know *you* mean it?"

"Tell you what. When you see all the stuff you and your parents asked for arrive, then you can decide if I'm telling the truth," Fletcher proposed.

"Fair enough," agreed Brian, and held up his hand to shake on it. On his way out he paused, then came over to place his arms around Adair's neck and kiss her cheek. "G'night, Adair. Sleep tight."

"Goodnight, Brian," she said with a warm hug.

Fletcher shut the door after Brian and stood over

Adair, slipping off his khaki jacket. "You always surprise me," she said, leaning back on an elbow.

"Then maybe you need to get to know me a little better," he replied with a wry smile as he climbed onto the bed.

Several hours later Adair gradually woke, hazily aware of movement around her. She shifted, reaching for Fletcher in the darkness. His side of the bed was empty.

Then from across the room he said quietly, "Time to get up, Adair. We're leaving."

# 2

A dair sat up groggily. "Leaving? Now? What time is it?"

"Shortly after two," Fletcher whispered. He pulled back the window curtains to look out to the street. Having seen what he wanted to see, he let them drop back and whispered, "Let's go."

"Okay, okay," she muttered, pulling her dress on over her head. "Can I stop by the restroom first?"

"Of course," he said indulgently. "You've got thirty seconds."

"Good grief, what's the rush?" she complained, hurrying down the hall, but she really did not have to ask. She was as relieved as anyone that they would not have to stay here any longer. She did not bother turning on the bathroom light and made it out in twenty-three seconds.

Fletcher paused at another door down the hall and opened it. Adair followed him into Brian's room, gingerly stepping through the minefield of toys on the floor. Fletcher laid a hand on the sleeping boy's chest. "Brian. Brian."

"Uhh?" the boy grunted, barely awake.

"Brian, Adair and I are leaving now. I wanted to tell you goodbye. Remember our deal," Fletcher said in a normal voice.

"Okay," Brian replied clearly, then rolled over.

Fletcher and Adair went back out into the hall, then tiptoed to the front door. They stepped out into the cool early hours of Halloween and Adair began shivering. As Fletcher locked the door behind them, she spotted a car with its lights off idling on the street—a sleek black Lincoln Mark.

Fletcher took her arm and hustled her toward the car. He yanked open the back door and shoved her inside. As he jumped in beside her and shut the door, someone ran out of the house across the street. "Go," Fletcher said, and the Mark took off.

Groping for a seat belt as the car rounded a corner, Adair braced herself with a hand on the front seat and looked at the driver—a slender African-American in a nice tweed jacket. When he glanced grinning into the rear-view mirror, Adair exclaimed, "Harle!" He had been her personal bodyguard assigned by Fletcher, unknown to her until his assignment had ended.

"Nice to see you, Mrs. Streiker," he acknowledged in the mirror as he smoothly guided the car up the access ramp to the freeway.

"Harle Kellum, you call me Adair. I never thought I'd see you again! How did you know—was he the one you called from the pay phone?" she turned to ask Fletcher.

"Yeah. Did you send Gordie for the chopper?" Fletcher asked him, and he nodded. "I like to keep Harle apprised when I'm in an area where I don't have any other contacts. But now I have Brian," he said in satisfaction, then leaned his head back with a weary yawn.

He pulled her closer to him. Bands of light from the freeway lamps passed so rapidly through the car that she could not get a reliable look at his expression. "Brian? He's just a kid. What good will he do you?" Adair asked.

Fletcher smiled cagily. "Everybody underestimates the kids because they sell themselves so cheaply. I bought his unquestioning devotion for a sixty-dollar car. Now I'll train him and put him to work for me."

"What about my mom and Dale? Can you use them?" she wondered.

"Um, I don't know, love. Let's see what they do with what they get." He gathered her up tightly and rested his cheek on her head, closing his eyes.

Adair turned to look at Harle's eyes in the rear-view mirror. He was watching the road ahead with a knowledgeable half-smile. Grunting irritably, Fletcher repositioned her head against his shoulder and settled back to sleep. So did Adair.

A few hours later, Harle had delivered them to the entrance of the parking garage at the Streiker Building in downtown Dallas. Adair leaned sleepily against Fletcher as he punched in the code to open the security gate, installed just that day after a recent bomb scare.

"Now, the code to this gate is—" He paused, observing her inattentiveness. "Uh, never mind. You're not likely to ever need it," he amended.

"Uh-huh," she nodded, eyes closed.

At the far end of the garage were the elevators.

Fletcher used his key in the one elevator which would take them all the way up to the penthouse, where he maintained an apartment. Adair stumbled into the apartment and back to the bedroom, crawling under the covers, hardly opening her eyes. By the time Fletcher had made a phone call and come to bed, she was fast asleep.

Late that morning Adair was awakened by the light streaming in from the skylights over the bed. She was so glad to have gotten that obligatory visit to Longview out of the way and be back in her own home. Stretching contentedly, she shifted under Fletcher's arm, which was draped across her ribs. She kissed his bare tanned shoulder and he mumbled something. Then she lifted the covers to look underneath them. With a wicked grin she reached both hands under the covers.

Fletcher sprang up and grabbed her. She laughed and pretended to resist, but he was not inclined to play games this morning. He calmly went after what he wanted until Adair yielded with a satisfied sigh.

Shortly thereafter they donned bathrobes to ransack the kitchen for breakfast. While Fletcher leaned into the refrigerator, Adair stood at the large sloped windows which faced westward. The Streiker Building was of modest height by Dallas standards—only thirty-three stories—but it was placed so as to provide a stunning westward view, particularly at sunset.

"I wish Sugar came on weekends," Adair sighed. She was referring to their housekeeper, though Adair had not viewed her in that light since the second hour of their acquaintance. She was a friend.

"We have to give Sugar some time with her own family," Fletcher said from the kitchen. "She always leaves something good. Here." He pulled out a platter of homemade cinnamon rolls and plucked off a note taped to the plastic wrap. "She says they're best heated up for about five minutes. Three hundred fifty degrees." He then bent and began scrutinizing the touch panels on the electronic oven.

Adair burst out laughing. "The billionaire entrepreneur and world traveler doesn't know how to operate his own oven!"

He turned wryly. "I'm not proud. Come show me how it works."

She swept into the kitchen. "You set it on bake, and enter the degrees and the time—" She did, but a beep signaled her error.

"Yes, Ms. Child?" he baited.

Frowning, she scrutinized the panel. "I know how to do this. I baked brownies in this oven."

"Sure you did," he said skeptically, lifting an edge of her robe.

"Fletcher!" she exclaimed. "Oh, I remember. You press *bake*, then enter the degrees and *start*—" The beep informed her of another error.

"I'd just as soon have them cold," he said, pulling out the coffee carafe to run water in it.

She studied the oven control panel in bewilderment a moment, then agreed, "I guess I would, too."

Even with cold rolls, the breakfast was cozy. They nestled together on a leather sofa with their coffee as an autumn rain began to pelt the windows. Fletcher glanced out the window, shuddering slightly. "I don't like winter in Dallas. It's cold and nasty." Then he casually remarked, "I have a few things to take care of this morning, then we'll fly out to Honolulu for our honeymoon. You'll love it there, and I'm anxious for you to meet my family."

"Sure," she said. Adair knew that his mother and sister lived there.

"So let's go get ready," he urged, getting up.

"I get the shower first," she claimed as he headed for the bedroom.

"Adair," he stated, turning back, "it's immoral to waste water when the shower's plenty big for two."

She pursed her lips and went to his side, but the telephone rang. Fletcher barely sighed and let go of her to answer it from the bedroom. "Hello. Yes, Yvonne. We got back in town early this morning. Yes? What?" Fletcher sat on the bed to listen.

"Paul Arrendondo has been calling, um?" he said thoughtfully. "Yes, I know about his work at the Phoenix Street Center in Fort Worth. Yes, I agree, he's been doing a remarkable job with the addicts; but—no. I've decided to cut off his funding."

Adair could almost hear Yvonne's protestations over the phone. Fletcher leaned back. "I know, Yvonne. I've seen his file. The answer is still no. I . . . understand that he's found another source of funding."

Adair leaned into the spacious tiled shower to go ahead and start the water, as it appeared that he would be on the phone with Yvonne for some time. Yvonne Fay was his personal assistant. To the rest of the world, she was merely a bookkeeper for the corporation, one of thousands of "little people." No one guessed her true status as right hand to the most powerful man in the Southwest.

Sure enough, Adair had showered, dried her hair, and dressed before Fletcher hung up the telephone. "Yvonne's got some things to cover with us before we leave, so she'll be coming up for a little while this morn-ing. She's already in the building. Why don't you let her brief you while I'm in the shower?" Fletcher said. "Oh, give her the list and the catalog in my jacket pocket. Tell her to give Brian's request priority."

"All right," she said, turning, but he caught her around the waist for a quick kiss.

The doorbell rang, and a faintly troubled look came across his face. "I was hoping to get away for some time with you before getting bogged down in business," he muttered. "I'm really anxious to get you out to the islands."

"One visit with Yvonne is not going to keep me from going to Hawaii," she declared. "Go shower." She shoved him lightly toward the bathroom and went to open the door. "Good morning, Yvonne," she said, smiling brightly.

Yvonne checked her rhinestone-studded watch. With her upswept blond hair and bulging briefcase, she looked crisp even in casual clothes, like the governor on vacation. "Technically, you're correct. Good morning, Adair. How was your visit with your family?"

"Not nearly as horrible as I thought it would be. Coffee?" she asked, moving toward the kitchen.

"One cup, thank you." Yvonne sat at the glass dinette in front of the sloped windows, placing the briefcase in a chair. "So have they changed, or you?"

"Neither," Adair replied, pouring a cup for Yvonne and herself. "They were exactly the same as always, except my little brother isn't a baby anymore. Fletcher being there is what made all the difference. No matter what they said, I didn't feel like I had to defend myself. It all just rolled off my back. Oh yes—I have something for you to take care of. Be right back." She set Yvonne's cup on the dinette and went to the bedroom to rifle Fletcher's jacket pockets. She noted the shower running as she went back out and shut the door.

"Before we had walked in the door Brian asked Fletcher to buy him a radio-controlled car," Adair said with an ironic smile. She laid the open catalog in front of Yvonne, who adjusted her designer glasses to look at it. "Fletcher told him yes, so my parents started hemming and hawing about needing stuff, and he told them to make a list."

Bridling her embarrassment over something she could not control, Adair laid out the list as well for Yvonne. "Fletcher asked that you take care of it. He said to give Brian's request priority."

Yvonne looked at the list, then up at Adair, then back down at the list. "Fletcher intends to buy everything on here for them? All at once?" Her voice was tinged with incredulity.

"That's what he said, yes," Adair related, glad that he was in the next room to confirm this insane request.

"My, my, my," Yvonne said in wonder. "It would be very interesting to know why he's doing that. Well. The car—the toy one—is to be sent first," she said, placing the list inside the catalog, and Adair nodded. "I'll take care of it," Yvonne said as she put the catalog in her briefcase.

"Yvonne, how are things at the Whinnets' house? What happened after Fletcher and I left the party?" Adair wanted to know.

Yvonne adjusted her glasses. "The paramedics came, but Darren was past saving. No one else was hurt. The police took a statement and left. Repair crews are out at the Whinnets' now—they should be completely done by the end of the day."

"As if nothing ever happened," Adair marveled. "They work on Sunday?"

"They work whenever Fletcher tells them to," Yvonne replied.

"Was there anything about it in the papers?" Adair asked.

"Yes, there was a rather subdued little article buried

in the second section of the *Expositor*. With everything else on my mind, I neglected to bring up a copy of the paper." Yvonne reached into her briefcase and withdrew an envelope. "Now, the first matter I need to cover with you is this letter from the Fort Worth Ballet."

She handed it over to Adair, who opened it with trembling fingers and read it silently while Yvonne sipped her coffee.

"Two weeks!" Adair gasped. "They're going to audition me in two weeks! How can I be ready in two weeks?"

"Ready for what?" Fletcher asked, coming from the bedroom. He was buttoning a fresh shirt which was losing some crispness due to the dampness of his hair.

Adair whirled toward him. "My audition with the Fort Worth Ballet!"

"In two weeks? Great," said Fletcher, smiling only with his lips.

"I have got to start conditioning classes immediately," Adair said, jumping up to the kitchen telephone to call Madame Prochaska.

"Adair," Fletcher said, "can it wait until we get back from Honolulu?"

She turned slowly back to him, her mouth dropping open. Wait! Wait? Every day that she delayed meant she would be that much less prepared. Every day she forwent practice meant relying that much more on his name rather than her own ability to land a spot in the corps. "Of course it can wait," she said hollowly.

His jaw tensed. "Tell me the truth, Adair."

"I am, Fletcher, honestly, it's just that . . . that I'm not in top form, and it's important that I get the position because I'm good and not because I'm married to you," she floundered.

"Is this more important than a honeymoon?" he asked. He was neither accusatory nor sarcastic; he was asking in order to get an answer.

"It's—" she lowered her head—"it's what I've dreamed of all my life."

"Then go ahead and make arrangements for classes," he said, sitting at the table with Yvonne. She immediately placed a pile of financial statements in front of him, and he pulled them toward him with a sigh which Adair did not hear.

She rushed to the telephone to call Madame Prochaska's studio. Adair knew that Madame would not be there, but at least she could leave a message—"Hallo?"

"Madame?" exclaimed Adair. "You're there! This is Adair Weiss—I mean, Streiker—and, Madame, I need your help! I've got an audition with the Fort Worth Ballet in two weeks!"

"Two weeks is not enough time," Madame said severely.

"I know, but it's all the time I've got. Will you help me get ready?" Adair asked plaintively.

"Come down to the studio today—now—and we will begin," Madame instructed.

"Thank you!" Adair exclaimed, and hung up.

She turned excitedly to Fletcher, but he had fire in his eyes. "Why didn't the audit catch this?" he was demanding of Yvonne, so Adair quietly slipped to the bedroom to get into her still-new dance gear.

After she had changed, she paused on her way out to slip an arm around Fletcher's neck and kiss his cheek. "Thank you," she whispered. He glanced up and nodded. "Bye!" Adair waved happily to Yvonne, who smiled, then she was riding down the elevator toward the long-delayed fulfillment of a dream.

Her little Mazda RX-7 was right there in the garage, where she usually parked. One of Fletcher's many anonymous employees must have returned it after the party where he'd made his surprise return. She hopped in and roared out of the garage and down the freeway toward the corner plaza where Madame Prochaska's dance studio was located.

Within fifteen minutes of departing the garage Adair was at the studio door. It was locked, so she leaned on the glass, knocking, until Madame came to unlock it. A lifelong dancer herself, she was a slender and sinewy forty-five-year-old, and Adair's instructor for the past three years. "Adair! Darling, come in."

"Thank you for seeing me on such short notice," Adair panted, swinging inside with her canvas bag.

"Of course, dear. I will cancel all the rest of my classes to work with you alone," Madame stated.

"Madame—that's wonderful! Would you really do that for me?" Adair said, overcome.

"Certainly, now that you can pay. A full day's instruction, each day will cost one thousand dollars," Madame added as she turned to the barre. "Time for warmups."

"A thousand dollars a day . . . ?" Adair repeated in shock.

"Your husband can afford that, no? He is very rich, no?" Madame said with arched, penciled brow.

"Yes, he is," Adair mumbled uncomfortably.

"We will begin now. First position," Madame said sternly, and Adair took her place at the barre.

They worked for the next five hours, first doing warmups, then practicing technique—Adair going over and over the same steps under her teacher's critical eye until Madame was satisfied with each muscle's contribution. For the final hour, Adair strapped on her toe shoes to practice *en pointe*. Finally, they ran through an entire dance number three or four times.

When Madame at last said, "That will be all for today," Adair almost dropped to the floor. "Much too out of shape," Madame uttered disapprovingly. "Tomorrow, be here at ten. We will begin then."

"All right, Madame. Thank you for your time," Adair groaned, though she felt that at a thousand dollars a day, thanks were superfluous.

Adair returned to a darkened, empty apartment. She halfheartedly looked for a note from Fletcher saying where he might be, but she would have been surprised to find one. "Maybe he's still working with Yvonne," she mused. She picked up the phone to call Yvonne's extension and reached her voice-mail.

Adair then tried calling Yvonne at home, but her answering machine came on. "He's likely to walk in before I get hold of her," she reasoned, so she dragged her aching muscles to the whirlpool tub.

Soaking, she began to wonder if Fletcher had gone on to Honolulu without her. "What a ridiculous idea—taking a honeymoon alone," she mused. She felt a stab of guilt when she recalled how anxious he had been to go. Also, he looked upset over what Yvonne had shown him. Something financial. What was that about an audit? "I should be learning about the corporation instead of jumping back into dance," she reflected. That was what Fletcher had seemed to expect—for her to become his business partner. She could hardly do that and spend the bulk of each day moving in front of a mirror, could she?

Adair inhaled. She just couldn't—she just wasn't able to—exchange her dream for yet another accounting class. Business was *so* boring. Even Fletcher's business, she was ashamed to admit.

Adair lolled around the apartment that evening waiting for Fletcher to come home so they could talk things through. But the recent strains on body and soul put her to bed hours before he came in.

The next morning was Monday, which meant that Fletcher hit the ground running. Adair knew that he had slept beside her last night because of the indention in his pillow, but he was not in the apartment when she ventured out of the bedroom.

Sugar was. "Good morning, Adair!" she said brightly from the kitchen. She was a pretty lady who wore her hair in fluffy white ringlets—Adair could never decide if Sugar got her nickname from her hair or her disposition.

"Good morning, Sugar." Adair smiled thinly, stretching stiff muscles. "Did you see Fletcher this morning?"

"No, I'm afraid he was up and gone before I got here at eight. I hope he had something more than coffee for breakfast. He gets so busy that he forgets to take care of himself as he should. Sometimes I'd get to worrying about him, the way he pushes himself. Honestly, a man who takes such good care of other people should take a moment for himself, shouldn't he? I'm so glad he has you. Now, he'll have to take a few days just to walk the beach and enjoy the sunset, won't he?" Sugar stated.

Adair opened her mouth, but Sugar's question was rhetorical. Her next one was not: "Would you like some cinnamon rolls? I'm sorry I can't make anything for you this morning—the oven's gone out again and I'm just furious over it."

"The oven isn't working?" Adair asked. "Well, that's why we couldn't heat up the rolls!"

"Yes, I've had problems with it several times before—a top-of-the-line model, can you believe it? We've had it repaired twice in the last eight months, but this time it's probably not worth trying to salvage. Fletcher will say it's time to start over with a new one," Sugar said decisively. "Coffee, dear?"

"Yes, thank you," Adair murmured. "Sugar, do you know where Fletcher will be today?"

"Have no idea," she said cheerfully, bringing the cup to Adair at the dinette. "Yvonne will know."

"I need to call her," Adair said suddenly, getting up.

She went to the kitchen phone and dialed Yvonne's office extension. "Bookkeeping. Yvonne Fay," she answered.

"Yvonne, I'm glad you're in. This is Adair."

"Yes, how are you this morning?" Yvonne asked.

"Um, fine. Yvonne, do you know where Fletcher will be today?" Adair asked.

Yvonne paused. "In town, I believe. Right now he's in a meeting with Charles Whinnet." He was one of a handful of Fletcher's confidential friends, and the president of the bank where Adair once worked. "Do you need to see him—right away?" Yvonne asked. There was something strained in her voice.

"Well, no, not really. I did want to see him later. I have to be at Madame Prochaska's at ten, and will probably be there for most of the day. Her private instruction is going to cost a thousand dollars a day," Adair told her with perhaps a twinge of bitterness.

"Do you need me to cut a check?" Yvonne asked.

"Why don't you—wait until I wrap up with her, and then pay her in one lump sum," Adair coolly suggested. "And be sure to deduct the four hundred I've already paid her."

"Will do," Yvonne said crisply. "Call me if you need anything else."

"Thank you," Adair said, then slowly hung up. Call Yvonne? How is it that things were settling into the very same routine as before, when Fletcher was gone? She had thought that after he returned, things would be different—that she wouldn't have to go through Yvonne for everything. But if she wanted him to be accessible to her, then . . . she had to be accessible to him, didn't she?

Adair went to the bedroom to put away her thoughts and put on her tights.

# ≈3≈

After a full day's workout, Adair dragged herself up to the apartment shortly before six that evening. Her muscles ached so unmercifully that it was all she could do to make it to the sofa nearest the door, so she might be excused for not noticing Fletcher standing in the kitchen. "Hello, Adair."

She was startled. "Fletcher! Oh, I'm so glad to see you!" She reached up from the couch and he came over to put his arms around her. "Not so tight, please," she gasped.

He eased back and said, "Sugar left a casserole for us. Are you hungry?"

"Famished!" she moaned. "So she must have gotten a new oven today."

Fletcher glanced back as he returned to the kitchen. "I don't know. She's had clearance to get one for months, but she kept trying to make do with the defective one." He began spooning out a plate for her.

Adair amended, "Just a little, please. I've got to drop a few pounds before the sixteenth." He nodded, shoveling some back into the casserole dish from the plate.

This he brought over and placed on the glass-topped coffee table. "Something to drink?" he asked her.

"Just water. Madame says I have to clear all the caffeine out of my system," she said. He drew her a glass of ice water and brought it to her, sitting beside her.

"Thanks," she sighed, taking up the fork. "Oh, my legs! Madame is trying to cram two months of workouts into two weeks. I wonder if that's such a good idea. Well, she must know what she's doing, she's been teaching for so long. So . . . how did your day go?" she asked, bringing up the glass.

He shrugged. "Regular day. Meetings and financials. Brian's car was delivered to him, by the way. Dana and Dale will begin receiving their deliveries tomorrow."

"That was very generous of you, Fletcher. I hope they appreciate it. Um, what was it that Yvonne showed you yesterday morning?" she asked. The casserole was delicious, but Adair made a mental note to ask Sugar to cook more low-calorie dishes.

He barely looked up as he chewed on a bread stick. "Yesterday? She covered eight or ten concerns with me then."

"Oh, that about the audit," Adair clarified.

Fletcher shifted, rubbing his face. "It's kind of complicated. I'd rather not rehash all that right now."

"I see," Adair said.

There followed a rather long silence. Fletcher finished his bread stick and leaned forward on his knees. Adair put down her fork and reached over to rub his shoulders. He closed his eyes, straightening to give her a better angle. "You're all knotted up," she observed.

"Just tired," he said in a low voice. "Running this

company gets to be like wrestling an octopus. There are other things I'd rather be doing."

Adair shifted closer to him. He turned under her hands with something like pain in his eyes. But before she could question it he had wrapped his arms around her for a hungry kiss, laying her back on the couch. "Fletcher!" she gasped as her right thigh cramped painfully.

He interpreted it as a rebuff and got up from the sofa to take her plate to the kitchen. "Fletcher—" But then the telephone rang.

"Hello," he answered tightly. "Yes." He stroked his forehead as he listened. "Oh, really? For how much?" he asked through gritted teeth. "Forget it, Chuck. I'm not giving that petty little despot Kurtz one tiny piece of it. He just irritates me, but he makes life horrific for the people under him. Who else . . . ? Yeah, we'll talk about the others. Okay, I'll meet you in half an hour."

He hung up and took up a light jacket lying across the sofa. "I'm going to meet with Chuck Whinnet for a while."

Adair stood unsteadily. "I'd like to go, too."

He paused. "Would you? It may take hours."

"That's okay." Smiling, she began to step away from the sofa but hit her shin on the coffee table instead. "Ow!" The pain bent her double and set off another cramp which caused her to buckle onto the couch.

Fletcher inhaled and looked away. "I think you'd better go soak in a hot tub instead. Don't . . . wait up for me." He turned and walked out.

Despondently, Adair went to the bathroom to run her water. As she watched it gush into the large marble tub, she fretted "Why isn't this working out? Why do I feel so guilty? Fletcher *told* me I could pursue dance now—he's the one who set it up! Why should I feel bad about taking advantage of what he offered?"

As she eased into the whirlpool tub, anger seeped into her thoughts. "He *said* I could take dance now, but he didn't really mean it. If he meant it, he'd be more supportive instead of making me feel guilty for working so hard at it. He just wants me at his beck and call every moment!"

She fumed in this manner for a while, but as the warm water drained the tension from her muscles, she found nothing left to support her anger. Nothing he had done suggested hypocrisy or ulterior motives. Could she blame him for wanting her by his side? Running the company was stressful, and he needed help with it. But Adair did not know how to tell him that she didn't *want* to sit through meetings and pore over financial reports.

"Okay," she argued with herself, "he doesn't have to be a great genius to figure out that you're not interested in shuffling paper. But management requires more than that—it requires dealing with people, and people have always been most important to Fletcher. So the hours you are home, you need to let him know that you care. You need to be supportive of *him*."

In that spirit, Adair was determined to wait up for him, but nodded off around 11:30 that night. And the following morning he was up and gone long before Adair stirred out of bed.

As a matter of fact, the next several days established the routine of Fletcher rising early, Adair rising late; then Adair working out all day with Madame Prochaska and seeing Fletcher for a few minutes in the evening, if at all.

When she did see him, she tried hard to be cheerful and interested. But she was preoccupied with ballet, he with matters she knew nothing about, so their shared ground for conversation shrank to almost nothing. Adair knew Fletcher could not be very happy with the situation, but she told herself there was nothing else she could possibly do. So it continued.

That Friday morning before she left for her workout (which was getting more tolerable each day), Adair got a call from Yvonne. "Your mother called trying to reach Fletcher, and he asked that you return her call," Yvonne relayed over the telephone. Sugar was dusting the curio shelves laden with the artifacts Fletcher had collected on his travels.

"Sure," Adair said, glancing at the clock. "I have a few minutes. Give me her number."

Yvonne did, and Adair called immediately. "Hi, Mom. What did you need?"

"Adair!" Dana said tearfully. "This is a mess—it's just a mess, and I don't know what to do!"

"What's a mess? What's the problem?" Adair asked in concern.

"*Your* husband sent all these things! They all arrived one right after another—bang, bang, bang. The car and pickup are in the driveway 'cause we don't have room in the garage. The city is threatening to issue a citation because this boat is sitting in front of our house on the street. People are here, swarming all over day and night, looking and ringing the doorbell and asking questions that are none of their business. It's horrible! It's got to stop!" Dana burst into tears.

"Well, what did you expect? You asked for all those things, didn't you? And Fletcher told you he'd send them, didn't he?" Adair said, irritated.

"But—we didn't expect it to be like this!" Dana whined.

"What do you want me to do, Mom? Take them back?" Adair asked.

"No!" exclaimed Dana. "But we've got to—no! Go away!" she shouted at someone away from the phone. "We need storage facilities for the boat, and an unlisted phone number, and private security people—"

"Didn't Fletcher send you fifty thousand for incidentals like this?" Adair asked impatiently.

"Well, yes, but we need more," Dana said falteringly.

"No, Mom, you don't need more. You can't even handle what you've got," Adair retorted.

"You ungrateful child! You've ruined our lives! You and that rich man! We're going to tell everyone where he lives and what he looks like, so he'll know what it's like to have people hounding him day and night asking for everything in the world!" Dana cried, then slammed down the receiver in Adair's ear.

Adair hung up and fumed to Sugar, "I knew that would happen! Fletcher gave them just what they asked for and they turn around and blame him for it!" She stalked back toward the bedroom to begin getting ready. "They're being greedy and irresponsible, then they're surprised to find out they're not happy! They wouldn't be happy no matter *what* Fletcher did for them!"

Adair halted near the bedroom door as the words boomeranged and hit her right in the face. Sugar, strangely, said not a word, but quietly continued dusting the shelves. Adair lowered her eyes, then went on into the bedroom to change into her tights.

⌒

The days passed in a blur of music and motion. Madame Prochaska selected a segment from *The Firebird* for Adair to perform at her audition. They readied a tape with the background music and finalized plans with the ballet's artistic director for Adair to audition in the auditorium of a community college halfway between Fort Worth and Dallas. The director assured Adair that she was receiving no special considerations; they would be auditioning several dancers at that time.

As the day approached, Fletcher melted into the background until he was almost invisible to her. She went without seeing him for days at a time, and did not even talk to Yvonne much. Adair's earlier concerns about how to fit into the management of his business also faded. Waking or sleeping, she thought of nothing but dance and the opportunity before her.

The evening before her audition, Adair came home to find Fletcher sitting at the glass dinette with reams of spreadsheets, a laptop computer, and a calculator in front of him. When she approached, he shoved them away and looked up. "Hi." He glanced at his watch, as it was almost eight o'clock.

"Hi!" She dropped into his lap to kiss him, then explained, "I didn't think you'd be here, so Madame and I had a bite to eat at the studio. She wanted to go over some of the finer points of conveying attitude." As she talked, she combed her fingers through his hair.

"Oh." He closed his eyes and laid his head on her chest. It was the movement of someone under a heavy load.

"I'm so nervous I can hardly stand it. I'll never be able to sleep tonight," she said breathlessly.

"Your audition's tomorrow?" he asked, lifting his head.

"Yes. At ten. Oh, Fletcher, do you think you can come watch? It would mean so much to have you there!" she exclaimed.

"That . . . won't be possible, Adair. But I hope it goes well," he said quietly.

"Thanks," she said halfheartedly. She wanted him to know that she was disappointed in him.

They didn't talk much after that, and when she went to bed that evening, he was still staring at the spreadsheets strewn across the table.

In accordance with her usual response to stress, Adair overslept the following morning. She had barely time to put up her hair and grab her canvas bag and tape player before waving goodbye to Sugar and flying down to her car.

The Tuesday morning traffic in downtown Dallas gave her some tense moments, but she made up for the time by going eighty miles per hour on the freeway to the community college, and arrived at the auditorium parking lot with minutes to spare.

She entered the auditorium to find three people waiting near the stage. One man turned. "Adair?"

"Yes. Jerrod?" she asked. He was the ballet company's artistic director. Nodding, he leaned forward to shake hands.

He was lean and casually dressed, with a studious Continental demeanor. "Let me introduce Angela, my assistant, and Dr. Miles Rutherford, chairman of the board of this college, which is a major supporter of our company."

"How do you do," Adair smiled, shaking the chairman's hand. He was a man whose appearance screamed *important,* and she naively wondered why he would be interested in auditioning dancers.

"I am so very pleased to meet you, Mrs. Streiker. This is a privilege and the beginning of what I hope to be a long and profitable relationship for all concerned," he effused.

Adair blinked at him, but the director's next words made the situation much clearer to her: "Will your husband be coming today, Adair?"

"He wanted to, but unfortunately, it was impossible. He's been extremely busy," she apologized.

The chairman glanced at the director. "I trust things are going well with his company," Dr. Rutherford hinted. Adair looked at him blankly. "I mean, that it is on solid ground, financially," he clarified.

Adair laughed outright. "On solid ground? Fletcher's company? An earthquake couldn't shake it!"

The others relaxed. "Of course. We felt so," the chairman agreed solicitously.

"Well, Adair, are you ready to dance?" the director asked, flashing a smile.

"Yes, I am," she said with bravado, hoisting her boom box to the edge of the stage. While the men sat in the second row, Adair slipped her jeans off from over her tights and tied on her toe shoes. Then she stood at the center front of the stage, poised to begin, and nodded at the assistant.

Angela pushed *play* and sat. The music started and Adair began to dance. Her years of discipline and instruction bolstered her two-week cram course, and she felt her confidence heighten as she executed perfect arabesques and pirouettes.

In two minutes it was all over. Adair took her bow and looked up; Jerrod and Dr. Rutherford immediately stood and applauded. A few beats later, Angela stood and brought her hands together as well. Adair watched her.

"Wonderful, wonderful, Adair!" Jerrod enthused.

"Lovely," Dr. Rutherford agreed. Angela was silent.

"We will be looking for you at our studio tomorrow morning at eight sharp. It won't cause any difficulties for you to come to Fort Worth every day, will it? Perhaps you'll want to maintain an apartment there.

I'm certain we can work something out. Please do bring your husband any time that he can get away. We are anxious to show him our little shop," Jerrod said smoothly, patting her on the back. Adair nodded vaguely, looking at Angela.

"I'm delighted to have had this opportunity to meet you, Mrs. Streiker. I look forward to seeing you and your husband again very soon," Dr. Rutherford said, shaking her hand vigorously.

Adair looked around distractedly, as they appeared ready to leave and there was no one else in the auditorium. "I thought you had several to audition," she mentioned.

Jerrod glanced at the chairman. "They . . . canceled," he said, then briskly added, "Tomorrow at eight." He leaned over and pecked her cheek. "You were enchanting. Come, Angela."

As the young assistant trotted after Jerrod and Dr. Rutherford, she shot a look at Adair that plainly said, *You weren't that great.*

Left alone in the auditorium, Adair slowly sat to take off her toe shoes. "I should have known," she whispered. "This wasn't about me at all. I could have spun on my rear and they would've accepted me." She paused to cover her eyes in despair. "How badly am I fooling myself here?"

She had no answers, so she dismally packed up her shoes and headed out. In the hallway outside the auditorium, she briefly looked up at a bulletin board she passed, and one large word caught her eye: "DANCERS."

Adair stopped to read the hand-printed announcement: "DANCERS. New Dallas-based ballet troupe auditioning dancers from 8–12 on Nov. 15 and 10–3 on Nov. 16, Green Room of the Sheraton Inn on LBJ." Adair squinted at the card. Today was the final day of auditions. They were auditioning right now.

In sudden resolve, Adair hurried out to her car and threw her things on the seat. She started it up and gunned it out toward the expressway, heading for Dallas.

Within thirty minutes she was pulling up to the Sheraton Inn. Carrying her canvas tote and her boom box, she shyly entered and asked a clerk for the location of the Green Room. She was directed down the corridor to a crowded room with a small wooden stage. A dancer was at this moment performing her routine, and a long line of hopefuls stood by for their chance to go on.

"Name?" Adair looked down at the questioner, a woman sitting tiredly at a folding table.

Adair opened her mouth and said, "Danielle Weiss." She wasn't exactly lying; that was her middle name and her maiden name. Mrs. Fletcher Streiker might be accepted in any ballet company she wished to join, but would Danielle Weiss?

"Have you got your own music of no more than three minutes?" the woman demanded.

"Yes." Adair nodded for emphasis.

"Okay, you're number one fourteen. You gotta wear the number during your audition," she said, ripping off the large paper tag at the perforations. "You got about an hour's wait. If you're not here when your number's called, then you go back to the end of the line," she droned.

"Okay. Thanks," Adair said, taking the number. She went to an empty folding chair and sat to watch number eighty-seven perform her audition. A bearded man and an aging ballerina sat at a table littered with scoresheets, watching intently. Eighty-seven was good, Adair judged, but she had a bad habit of tilting her head that would probably render her unacceptable.

For the next hour and a half Adair watched dancers audition. The vast majority of them were girls, all of them most likely younger than herself. Twice Adair got up to leave, but each time she sat back down. She had to know whether she was really good enough to dance professionally. After making up her mind to actually go through with this audition, she darted out to the hotel's coffee bar for a snack to bolster her. Then she returned to watch some more.

When they got to number 106, Adair moved to a corner of the room to do warmups. At number 109, she put on her toe shoes and practiced a troublesome arabesque *allongee*. Then the moment came. "One fourteen," the bearded man called, looking around.

Shaking, Adair went up and placed her tape player on their table. "Danielle Weiss?" he asked. She nodded, forcing a smile, and took the stage.

"Are you ready?" the woman asked. Adair nodded again, lifting her chin, and the woman started the tape. Adair blocked out everything but the music and began to dance.

Mingling her movements with the music transported her as only dance could do, and in a sudden moment of clarity she saw Fletcher in her mind. He looked tired and lonely—and where was she?

With a burst of yearning Adair realized where she had gone wrong here. Dancing was not an end in itself; it was valuable only as an expression of love. That's what she had wanted to begin with, and had somehow lost sight of: to dance for him. What good was dancing when she had to shuck him aside to do it?

Adair finished her dance and bowed. The woman clicked off the tape player and said, "Number one fifteen." Numbly, Adair retrieved her boom box and sat to remove her toe shoes. She was so depressed that one tear escaped down her cheek before she could stop it.

She packed everything in her canvas tote and slung it over her shoulder to leave. Wiping her eyes clean, she paused in front of the woman by the door to ask, "When will they announce who made it?"

The woman glanced at her watch. "Another hour and they'll finish auditions. They'll announce selections immediately after." Adair hesitated, then decided, *What the heck; I'm here; I might as well wait.* So she sat toward the back and continued to watch. In her own mind she felt she was as good or better than anyone else she saw, but that did not provide much comfort. She no longer trusted her own opinions.

Finally, the last hopeful took her bow. The man and woman at the table put their heads together over their score sheets while the crowded room of aspiring dancers waited nervously.

Then the bearded man took a sheet with him to the stage, turned, and said, "Would the following please stay to meet with me and Marian for a few minutes: Mark Geraldi, Tammy Bains, Anselm Geraldi, Riley O'Shay, Danielle Weiss, Peter Bonham, and Leslie Dahl."

The select few darted through the largely disappointed crowd like salmon leaping upstream while Adair sat like a rock. "I made it," she breathed in disbelief. "I made it."

In a trance, she slowly made her way forward as the bearded man was lecturing the new recruits: "We will expect nothing less than total commitment from you. Your lives will be geared to dance and nothing else. You will live it and breathe it and sacrifice anything else that gets in the way of your ability to perform. Now— Ms. Weiss?"

The other dancers stared at her as Adair broke from the tight circle to start out of the room. "I'm sorry," she smiled, shaking her head, "but I can't give you what I owe someone else. Thanks. Goodbye."

She walked out of the room on clouds of joy. Someday she would dance—she would—but it would be in such a time and place that suited the one who made it possible. Meanwhile, she would learn whatever was necessary to be able to help Fletcher however he needed her. "Even if I drown in spreadsheets!" she vowed.

Passing through the hotel lobby, she glimpsed the newspaper racks and paused. Was it because she was thinking about him that she thought she saw his name in the headlines?

Adair stopped and dug a quarter from her change purse to shove in the slot and open the rack. She lifted out a newspaper and unfolded it. The headline on the lower half of the paper read: "Streiker Corp. Breaking Up."

The headline might as well have been in Arabic, as incomprehensible as it was to Adair. She read it three times before it began to sink in. The story below it began:

The Dallas-based Streiker Corporation is in the process of being dismantled and sold, insiders reported late Monday afternoon. Apparently due to his frustration with mismanagement and illegalities by a number of division heads, company founder and chairman Fletcher Streiker has decided to liquidate the company. Details were sketchy at press time, but persistent rumors as to the company's future have been confirmed by three sources who spoke on the condition of anonymity. The reasons behind such a drastic step are unclear, and Streiker did not return numerous phone calls requesting comment for this article. A meeting of top executives reportedly will be held Tuesday morning to finalize plans to sell off assets.

The article went on to trace the company's development by the reclusive Streiker, who

will be severely affected, if not impoverished, by the demise of the company bearing his name. Experts estimate the loss suffered due to mismanagement to exceed half a billion dollars. Repayment of debts could consume as much as $1.7 billion. Unfavorable publicity surrounding the corporation could result in additional billion-dollar losses on paper. As the corporation has been the major vehicle of Streiker's philanthropy, the total amount of which is beyond calculation, city leaders expressed surprise and dismay at the collapse of such a powerful business empire.

Heartsick, Adair laid down the paper. The money meant nothing to her—what nauseated her was the thought of Fletcher bearing this crushing burden alone while she traipsed to dance every day. With renewed urgency, Adair hurried to her car to go home.

Some minutes later she wound her way through traffic into the garage of the Streiker Building and parked. It was crowded with throngs of people—seeing cameras, Adair suspected reporters. Leaving her dance gear in the car, Adair casually got out and sauntered to the elevators.

Somebody in the crowd recognized her, and all at once they were surging forward, shouting questions. The elevator opened and Adair managed to get in and use her penthouse key before anyone else could reach her.

The apartment was empty. Heart pounding, Adair went to the bedroom and dropped onto the bed, plucking up the telephone. She dialed Yvonne's extension and waited tensely.

When Yvonne answered, Adair felt a flood of relief. "Oh, thank goodness you're there," Adair breathed. "Yvonne, I just saw the headlines in the paper about the company—I'm so ashamed that I haven't talked to Fletcher—I didn't know—"

"I'm sorry, Adair. I tried to reach you, but I didn't know where you were. Fletcher does not have Harle following you around anymore." Yvonne's voice was very low.

"Where is he?" Adair asked. "Wherever he is, I need to see him right away. I'll go to him."

Yvonne inhaled, and when she spoke again, her voice was trembling. "I'm sorry," she repeated. "Fletcher's mother suffered another heart attack and died very suddenly today. We could not find you, so Fletcher flew out to Honolulu by himself for the funeral."

"No," Adair whispered, slipping from the bed to the floor. "Oh no, no."

"I don't know when he'll be back. He . . . did not leave any instructions for you," Yvonne said as gently as possible.

"No, no, no," Adair sobbed. She curled up beside the bed in grief, unconsciously hanging up the phone. "Oh, Fletcher, I'm so sorry. I'm sorry. What can I do? What will I do without—" She broke off and looked up, staring into the vacant bedroom. What was that she heard?

The sound became unmistakably louder, and Adair's head jerked up toward the ceiling. It was a helicopter, coming closer. Now it was right overhead. Fletcher had a landing pad on the roof of this building.

Adair leaped up and bounded over the bed. She flew out the door and up the stairwell to the rooftop. Bursting out onto the roof, she saw a red and white helicopter settle on the pad, rotors spinning. Fletcher leaned out of the pilot's seat.

She reached him in several long, graceful strides and jumped up to hold him while crying copiously. "Go pack!" he shouted over the roar of the rotors.

She babbled refusals, clinging to him, but he insisted, "Hurry and pack a bag! I'll wait! Go!"

"You'll wait?" she cried dubiously.

"Yeah, for thirty seconds," he grinned, and the sight of it filled her heart.

"Be back in twenty!" she shouted, sprinting back to the stairwell door.

She scampered down to the apartment just as Sugar entered with a handful of mail. "Sugar—Fletcher's waiting—I've got to pack," Adair panted.

"I just knew you'd be back in time! I've got your bags ready to go. They're sitting in the closet," Sugar said triumphantly.

"I love you, Sugar!" Adair exclaimed, kissing her cheek. She ran into the bedroom, threw open the closet doors, and seized the two tapestry-covered suitcases that sat waiting. She'd never seen these particular bags before, but hardly stopped to question where they came from.

"Take this, too!" Sugar thrust a letter to Adair, who gripped it between two fingers as she ran past. "And have a good trip!"

"Thanks!" Adair's voice echoed from the stairwell.

Adair threw her bags into the small space behind the two seats in the helicopter, where two black leather suitcases already sat. She plopped into the passenger seat and leaned over for an ardent kiss from the pilot. He held her with one arm while buckling her seat belt with the other. Then he sat back, smiling, to raise the collective pitch lever and they lifted off.

She picked up the headset at her elbow, looking down at traffic snarled far below them around the Streiker Building. Adair put on the headset, testing it, "Fletcher?"

"Hi," he said through his headset, expertly guiding the chopper westward.

"You came back for me," she said, blinking to keep her eyes clear.

"I was almost to the airport when Reggie radioed that you were in," Fletcher replied. Reggie, a security guard, was just another employee doing his job.

"Oh, Fletcher," she reached over to stroke his shoulder, and he kissed her hand. "I'm so sorry about your mother."

In reply, he merely nodded. Biting her lip, she went on, "It's my fault that you didn't get to see her before she died. If we had left right away when you wanted to, you would have had time—"

"What?" he said. "I can't hear you."

"I said—," she began, adjusting the microphone closer to her lips.

"I don't hear you at all," he interrupted. She fell silent, knowing the only reason he did not hear her was because he chose not to.

Then she looked down at the letter which lay crinkled between her fingers. She smoothed it out, saying, "Sugar gave me this letter as I ran out—it's from Brian!"

He glanced over. "Good. Hold on to it for me."

Smiling wryly, Adair twisted to unzip a suitcase and stuff the letter inside. But there was another concern which had to be voiced, another area in which she had failed him. "Fletcher, I saw the newspaper headlines about the company this morning. I had no idea—"

"We'll have to talk about that later," he said, flipping on the radio. He called for clearance to land, and was directed to a heliport at Love Field. This smaller airport was in the middle of Dallas, but Adair had never taken a plane from it before.

He set the helicopter down smoothly and a maintenance man in coveralls came running up. He quickly helped Adair out and then reached back for all four suitcases—two in each hand. Adair was manually guided to a cart with a waiting driver. Their bags were tossed in the back; Fletcher threw himself onto the seat beside her and the cart took off with a lurch.

They were driven right up to a waiting 727, which they promptly boarded. No lines, no tickets, no metal detectors. Dazed, Adair sat in a plush seat and fastened her seat belt. In a matter of minutes the plane was taxiing toward takeoff. Fletcher appeared from the cockpit and sat next to her, buckling his seat belt.

"So," he said, "how'd the audition go?"

She blinked at him, then lowered her eyes in shame. "They accepted me all right, but the main reason they were interested in me was to get money out of you." Gathering steam: "I had to know if I was any good or just fooling myself, so I went to another company's audition, and I made it."

He nodded reflectively. "I wondered what took you so long. When do you start?"

"I'm not," she said. "I told them I wasn't interested. There are more important things I need to be doing."

Fletcher studied her. "If you don't take this opportunity to dance, chances are that not even I could make another one for you later."

She shook her head resolutely. "That doesn't matter. It's not that important to me anymore."

But Fletcher did not look happy or grateful. "Do anything you want, but don't blame me. I don't care what anybody else says about me, but I won't have you blaming me because you never got to dance. Are you sure about this, Adair?"

At first she was hurt, until she thought about her own fickleness and tendency to lay blame. "I'm sure I love you, Fletcher. And it's time for me to give you the same consideration you've been giving me. Or at least try," she said humbly.

That is when he smiled, his eyes crinkling just slightly in a manner that reflected the depth behind them. She took in everything about his face—the full lips and black hair, the golden-brown complexion—and thought, *I'd love you if you didn't have a dime.* Then her heart sank to realize that soon, he may not.

"I read about the company shutdown in the papers this morning. Fletcher, I . . . I don't know what to say. Whatever happens, I'll be right by your side," she said quietly.

Whereupon he put his head back and laughed. Stunned, Adair watched him explode in a good, head-clearing belly laugh. "You mean you'd love me even if I couldn't whisk you to Honolulu on a private jet?" he asked, wiping his eyes.

Adair had just about decided to get mad when he took her hand and kissed it. "I'm sorry, babe. I don't mean to make light of you. Your loyalty is just about the most important thing in the world to me. It's just that—gee, Adair, you of all people should know not to believe everything you read in the papers."

"Then, it's not true?" she asked hopefully.

"No, it's true," he said. She gazed at him in bewilderment as he kissed her fingers, one at a time, starting with the pinky, smiling all the while. "But it's not *quite* the end of the world," he added slyly.

"I see that I missed a lot over these past two weeks," she noted coolly. "Would you care to bring me up to date?"

"Delighted," he grinned. "Fact is, the Streiker Corporation has outlived its usefulness. It's gotten too big, too bureaucratic, too inefficient . . . too publicized and tainted. I've tried restructuring it, but there's too much internal resistance and outside interference. So I'm scrapping it and starting over," Fletcher told her. "Chuck is overseeing the sell-off, which will take somewhere between eighteen months and two years. After that, we'll operate in a new way. He and Yvonne will be my liaisons to fixed-asset managers, stockbrokers, and new ventures. I'll be invisible—I won't have any outward ties to their business, however they choose to structure it, so I'll get some of my freedom back."

"But—the paper said you'd be just about broke after the sell-off," Adair mentioned.

"I'm afraid their 'experts' don't have the vaguest idea how much I'm really worth," he said in satisfaction. "This isn't a fire sale. I have no debts. And I'm not going bankrupt." Adair was vastly more relieved than she cared to admit.

"Does it ever bother you," she wondered, "to see so many . . . untruths spread about you everywhere you look?"

"Well, sometimes," he admitted, "'cause then I have to spend so much time reeducating new employees. But to go around trying to correct all that misinformation would be a waste of time. People are going to think what they want to think. The only ones who are going to give me the benefit of the doubt are the people who know me, and when you get right down to it, they're the only ones whose opinions matter, anyway."

"The main thing I have learned about you," she said solemnly, "is that you have a very wicked sense of humor."

"Thank you," he acknowledged. "That reminds me—" He glanced at his watch and beckoned to the flight attendant, who brought over a telephone. Fletcher dialed and sat back. "Chuck? You can go ahead and place those divisions on the market that we talked about earlier. Right. Oh? What's that?" He listened for a few minutes, a shadow crossing his face. "Um-hmmm. Okay, let me think on that. I'll get back with you," he finally said, and laid the phone down on the table in front of them.

"What will happen to the employees in the divisions that you sell?" Adair asked with some trepidation.

"That depends on the new owners," Fletcher answered. "That's why I'm being picky about who I sell to."

"What about the Streiker Building?" she asked.

"It's being sold," he confirmed. "I told you that wouldn't be our permanent home."

"Sugar? And Reggie?" she asked, pained.

He looked at her. "What do you think, Adair? Do you think I'm putting Sugar out on the street?"

"No. You'll use her somewhere," Adair said.

"You bet I will. If the move wouldn't tax her health too much, I'd put her in my Los Angeles home," he said thoughtfully. "Anyway, yes—Chuck and Yvonne will invite a select few employees to apply for positions with their new firm. But even they won't know I'm behind it. Not at first."

"They'll guess," she speculated. "Especially with all

the postmortems being done on your old company."

Fletcher eyed her. "Funny you should say that. Chuck mentioned that some jackals have been lurking around to try to turn the sell off into a feeding frenzy. He said they've got to be distracted before he can make much progress." He closed his hands under his chin, staring intently into space. Adair laid her head contentedly on his shoulder.

Then her stomach growled and Fletcher looked down at her. Embarrassed, she admitted, "I haven't had much to eat today."

"All you have to do is ask," he said, gesturing to the flight attendant again.

They were brought a cold tray of hors d'oeuvres which they consumed, Adair eating half again as much as Fletcher (except for the shrimp, which she never particularly liked). But as the ham-and-cheese pinwheels reminded her of something Sugar would fix, she ate them all, worrying vaguely about where Fletcher would use Sugar, considering her arthritis.

When she could not eat another bite she said, "Thank you," pushing away the tray, and the flight attendant wordlessly removed it. "Oh, it feels so good to eat something without feeling guilty about it," she sighed, draping herself across Fletcher. "It feels so good to be where I'm supposed to be," she added in a murmur. He smiled, holding her.

She closed her eyes in another spate of self-affliction. "I can't stop thinking about your mother . . . another heart attack, after that coronary bypass. She wrote me such a sweet letter after you and I were married, and I never got to meet her. . . ."

"There's nothing to be done about that now, so don't whip yourself," he said softly. He leaned his head back and rubbed his eyes. "She . . . was ready. She missed

Dad, and she didn't want to be a burden to anyone. She just seemed to be hanging on long enough to make sure that I'd find someone to marry."

"Your mom went about it a lot better than my mom. Before I was out of high school, she was trying to set me up with the son of everyone remotely successful she knew," Adair said with irony. "You know that she called about a week ago?" she asked.

"That's right," he remembered. "What did she need?"

"To gripe and complain that you actually sent them all that stuff they asked for," Adair said.

"Hmm," he said, pulling out a small address book from his jacket pocket. "Guess I'd better see if I can help them."

"Fletcher, why bother?" she asked.

"You'll see." He picked up the phone and dialed a number, then listened for a moment before putting the phone back down. "They've switched to an unlisted number," he told her.

She could hardly restrain an I-told-you-so reaction, but before she said anything he requested, "Where is Brian's letter? Let's have a look at it."

Adair got up to pull one of the suitcases out of a compartment and open it. She found Brian's letter to Fletcher and brought it to him. Furrowing his brow, Fletcher ripped it open and held it out for her to read with him. It was written in pencil by a child's independent hand:

Dear Fletch,

That is a cool name so that is what I will write. My new car came and it is grate! It goes like nothing. I know you are telling the truth becos Mom and Dad got a bunch of stuff and they were happy like me, but then they got mad and hollered a lot. I stay out of the way and play with my car. I remeber that you tole me goodby and to remeber our deal but I thout I was dreeming. Then you were gone and I knew I was not dreeming. I can't wait for you to come!!

I love you.

Brian

Adair read the letter silently and then looked at Fletcher. Smiling, he laid the letter on the table and took out blank paper from a nearby compartment. He pulled out a pen from his jacket pocket and composed a reply:

Dear Brian,

I'm glad you are enjoying the car. It makes me happy to buy things for people who enjoy them. I am sorry that your mom and dad are having trouble with the things they wanted. If they will give me your new phone number, I'll call and see if I can help them.

Brian, you may hear people saying that I don't have any more money. Don't worry about it, because it isn't true. I am shutting down my company because it wasn't useful anymore. But I'm still working.

Adair and I are on our way to Hawaii to see my family. My sister needs me right now because our mother just died. Do you know what my sister calls me? Panny. Isn't that funny? I don't think I would let anyone but her call me that.

Well—Adair could if she wanted to, but thank goodness she hasn't. I love you, too, Brian.

Fletch

He folded the letter, sealed it in an envelope, and addressed it to Brian. Then he put Brian's letter in an envelope with a note to Yvonne, and addressed that to her. This he handed over to the flight attendant, who knew what to do with it without being told. Then Fletcher sat back with his arm contentedly around Adair.

"Well, Panny," she began, and he eyed her sideways. She grinned, then turned serious. "You told him a lot. What if someone else reads that letter?"

"I hope they do," he replied. "But, we'll see. . . ."

During the two-hour flight to the West Coast, Fletcher and Adair caught up on the intimate, relaxed conversations they had missed for the past two weeks. "I still can't get over your shutting down the company," she admitted. "I thought you wanted me to learn all about it so I could help you run it."

A strange expression flitted across his face. "I did want your help with my business, but I didn't mean the Dallas company. I have other business that's much more important to me than that. Actually, that's the main reason I was so anxious to get you to Hawaii."

"You have another business in Hawaii?" she asked, sitting up.

He paused. "I have . . . other business there, yes. And what I had in mind was your taking charge of that business."

Adair was gratified. "Are you sure I can? You know how weak my math is."

"You have superlative qualifications for this business," he said. "I made sure of that before I proposed to you. And it's far too important to me to let it slide another day."

"I'm intrigued! What is it?" she asked eagerly.

"I'll show you when we get there," he said, stroking her hand. Adair looked out the window as if gauging how long it would take them to reach Honolulu.

They landed at an airfield in San Francisco for refueling and maintenance. There, Fletcher took advantage of the stop to head straight for Fisherman's Wharf, and Adair had the pleasure of watching a seafood lover satisfy his craving for shellfish straight from the net.

It was dark outside, and as they sat in a restaurant which smelled of the sea, Adair stared dreamily at the lights reflected across the bay. She saw herself in a business suit, attended by scores of suited subordinates while she closed crucial deals for Fletcher.

After the requisite phone calls to Yvonne and Chuck, they reboarded the jet for Honolulu. As the trip would take four hours, Adair was gratified to find sleeping quarters made up in the jet's luxurious interior. It was a very pleasant flight—

Until it was time to disembark. When Fletcher woke her, she thought it was morning. But when they stepped off the plane, it was pitch black outside and airport traffic was sparse. Adair's body told her right then to go back to bed, but Fletcher was ebullient.

Someone from the grounds crew ran up to him with a set of keys, which Fletcher took straight to a waiting car—a black sports convertible. As he threw their suitcases in the back seat, Adair groaned, "What time is it, anyway?"

"Let's see—" He paused to reset his watch. "About four-thirty."

"In the morning?" she moaned.

But Fletcher was gazing upward. "Look at that moon!" It was nearly full, keeping the clouds back with its splendor.

Adair glanced up. "It's pretty," she admitted dully.

"Hop in," Fletcher said suddenly, and Adair plopped into the car as he cranked it up. He swung out to an empty thoroughfare with a specific destination in mind.

They passed through the bright lights of Honolulu, which showed activity even at this unheard-of hour, but Fletcher kept driving until the lights were extinguished by profuse tropical forests. A few minutes later he exited the highway down a narrow, winding road, heavily overgrown.

He parked in a cul-de-sac and hopped out. Adair slowly stepped out of the car, peering into the lush darkness around them. There was the roar of nearby rushing water. Fletcher took her hand and began sprinting up a path that had been invisible a moment before. She stumbled along, gripping his fingers, until they suddenly broke out into a clearing and she caught her breath in awe.

Illumined by moonlight, a silver waterfall cast itself continually over rocks fifty feet above their heads to crash into the deep grotto at their feet. The spray rose up like incense, like an aromatic prayer filling the air around the altar of rocks. Adair at once recalled seeing a picture of this waterfall in his file—but neither photographs nor words could capture the sense of being in the presence of preternatural majesty.

Fletcher regarded the waterfall almost as if he were communicating with it. Then he held her in his arms to put his mouth to her ear and say, "I can't even remember the first time I saw these falls. They're ingrained in me. Wherever I am, I can close my eyes and see them in detail. Then to come back here and see them just as I remembered—it's like stepping into something timeless."

Adair squeezed his hand. They wandered down fragrant paths where Fletcher seemed to greet old friends among the flora. Adair did not know the names of half the plants they passed, but she was impressed just the same. The leaves were commonly huge, fanning out like green doorways. They snuggled close together in every available inch of space. And the exotic flowers that peeked out everywhere made the air heavy with fragrance.

She stopped to touch a glossy red heart-shaped flower which looked like plastic. "Anthuriums," Fletcher told her. Even in the dim moonlight she could see them profusely covering the ground.

"They just—grow out here?" she marveled.

"All over," Fletcher said.

On down the path were soft pink orchids. "I've never seen these outside of a box," she said in wonder.

"This is how they were meant to be seen," he said, cupping a delicate blossom.

They walked on silently through ferns, tangerine trees, and birds of paradise. Then reluctantly he turned to guide her back out. When he ducked slightly on the path and twisted, she realized with a mild shock that they were trespassing through a breached fence. She consoled herself with the knowledge that they had harmed nothing and taken nothing—not so much as a single flower.

⌒

They returned to the car. After a last glance over his shoulder, Fletcher started the engine to roar off down one winding road and up another. Adair held her breath, wondering if he drove like this all the time. The headlights caught a sign—"Nuuanu Pali"—and Fletcher pointed off into the darkness. "Before we build, you might want to look at the house I have here. It's pretty nice."

"Would we live here?" she asked, holding her hair back from whipping in her face.

"I'm thinking about it," he responded. He looked so at home, so happy.

He rejoined the highway and took it inland as it rose higher and higher. The darkness began fading. Finally, he turned off at the summit and stopped the car. Adair climbed out, immediately overwhelmed. On one side she gazed down sheer rock cliffs that dropped a thousand feet to the foaming coast below. On another side were miles of verdant valley sprinkled with city lights and bordered by ancient volcanic mountains. Adair was struck speechless.

And then the sun rose.

**5**

Sunrise over Kaneohe Bay was almost overpowering in its breadth, depth, and reach. Adair had never witnessed such a consummate display in all her life—sky and sea became one vast carrier of the sun's luminance. And to think that it happened every single day was mind-boggling.

Shivering, she turned to Fletcher as he watched the common miracle unfold. Heedless of his jacket whipping in the brisk wind, he took in the spectacle with glazed eyes. It was a part of him, Adair understood. How a certain spot of real estate could have such a profound effect, she didn't know. But when you loved a place so, you carried it with you all your life like ballast through troubled seas.

Fletcher turned toward her, his shadow long and deep on the rock behind him. "You're cold," he said, shucking his jacket off to drape it over her shoulders.

"N-not really," she stammered, but accepted his

jacket anyway.

His hands rested on her shoulders as they continued to watch the sunrise. The stronger light enabled
Adair to see more detail in the expanse of greenness
below them: banana groves, buildings among the coastal
city lights, and the mountains beyond the bay. "I've
never seen anything like it," Adair confessed.

"There is nothing else like it," he said, regarding
the view. When the light was at its fullest, he turned
toward the car. "Time to go."

Adair crawled sleepily into the passenger seat,
unaware that he had allowed her to sleep for several
hours on the plane after they had landed. He started
the car and took off down the deserted highway.

Adair had just about nodded off when Fletcher suddenly pulled the car off the road beside a pay phone.
"It's early, but Desirée won't mind. I know she's anxious to meet you. Come here," he said, motioning her
over as he picked up the phone and dialed. "I want you
to talk to her, too." He cradled the receiver on his shoulder and pulled her close beside him. Adair would just
as soon have let him do all the talking, but in no way
was she going to rebuff his sister.

"Desirée!" Fletcher exclaimed happily when she
answered. "*Pehea oe*, baby girl?"

"Panny, where are you? Where have you been?
We've been waiting and waiting for you to come!" The
little girl voice was angry enough for Adair to hear.

"I'm on the island. I got here as soon as I could,"
Fletcher said, his voice dampening slightly.

"Mother waited *weeks* to see you—she hung on as
long as she could waiting for you to come see her. Why
did you have to wait until she died to come?" Desirée
demanded.

Adair winced. "Tell her it's my fault," she whispered.

Fletcher barely glanced up. "I couldn't get away, Desirée. It couldn't be helped. I'm here now."

"Well, that's great!" his sister shot back sarcastically. "Mother's death made the papers, so now every *malihini* around is parked in front of our house to get a shot of you! There's no way you can get close, Fletcher!"

"Well, I'll just come—," he began.

"*Aole!*" she objected vehemently. "The funeral's going to be enough of a circus as it is! *Don't come*, Fletcher! It won't do any good now!" She hung up in his ear.

Fletcher quietly replaced the receiver. "I'm so sorry. It's all my fault," Adair said miserably.

"Don't be ridiculous," he said absently. "She's upset because she and Mother were very close. Give her a few days to calm down and she'll be okay."

He leaned on the phone booth to think, then checked his watch. "I'll call Chuck a little later," he mused. "Give him more time to see what he can do. For now, let's go home for some breakfast." Morning was fully underway, and cars began appearing along the highway. Adair climbed in and Fletcher turned the car back toward Honolulu.

He exited on a road that wiggled its way up the lush tropical side of a mountain. It was the kind of drive one usually saw only in the movies or in a dream sequence. At periodic breaks in the greenery, Adair could look down over the whole city of Honolulu.

Fletcher turned off at a nearly invisible intersection and went up a rambling drive until a sprawling stucco house came into view behind an eight-foot fence. At the wrought-iron gate, he leaned out of the car to press buttons on a security panel, and the gate slowly opened. "Eight eight three four," he said. "Same as on our apartment door."

"This is your house?" she said in wonder.

"Yes," he said. He drove up the circular driveway, parked in front, and took their bags from the back seat.

Adair wandered up to the heavily scrolled front door. "What a beautiful house," she murmured.

"Thanks," he said, putting down an armload of bags to reach for the doorbell.

In a moment the door was opened by a Hawaiian woman in a flowing muumuu. She was very round and very brown. At the sight of Fletcher, she broke into a sardonic smile. "*Aloha*, Boss! Funeral today at ten. You here just in time."

"That I am," he said, hauling in their bags. "Adair, this is Nona."

"Hello," Adair smiled.

Nona looked at her out of the corner of her eye and muttered, "*Haole*."

Fletcher dropped the bags in a show of impatience. "Don't start, *wahine*; I'm *hapa-haole* myself and I didn't have to marry an islander."

"Don't get swell head, Boss; I say nuthin'," Nona insisted.

Adair picked up her own bags as Fletcher pointed past the adobe-tiled entrance to a gently curving wrought-iron stairway. "Well, get something on; we're hungry," he ordered over his shoulder.

"How do I know when you come? It's ready when it's ready," Nona huffed, swinging away.

As they climbed the stairs with their bags, Adair glanced down at Fletcher behind her. "She's not Sugar, is she?" she whispered.

He looked up with a wry smile. "No, she's not, but here, I need a Nona instead of a Sugar. Besides, she likes you."

"How can you tell?" Adair asked.

"She spoke, didn't she? You got a red-carpet welcome," Fletcher insisted.

Before she could comment on that, they had reached the top of the stairs. Fletcher leaned over to open a door off the hallway. Adair looked into an airy, tropical room with a canopy bed. One whole wall of the adjoining bath was built of glass blocks, and the shower was outside on a balcony. It was fenced in completely with bamboo, and the grounds beyond were heavily landscaped for privacy, but the sunshine reached down through the open top of the large stall.

As Adair stood gazing into the open shower, Fletcher came up from behind, reaching around her to unfasten the top buttons on the loose blouse that covered her leotard. "Want to try out the shower?" he suggested. Interested, Adair set down her suitcases.

She found that she enjoyed showering in the sunshine, lathering up with natural sponges and tropical soap, rinsing under sparkling streams of water. When Fletcher started carrying her to the bed they were both dripping wet, so she managed to grab a towel off the rack on the way. But somehow they got sidetracked from drying each other off and the sheets took up most of the moisture.

While they were enjoying themselves in this manner, Nona's voice suddenly boomed from just outside the door: "*Hele mai ai!*"

"What—?" Adair gasped, scrambling for the top sheet.

Fletcher lay back and laughed, shaking moisture from his damp hair. "She has breakfast ready. C'mon, I'm starved." He got up from the bed to open a large freestanding wardrobe and toss her a gauzy dress.

Adair barely hesitated over its sheerness before she accepted it, reasoning that no one was here but the housekeeper, anyway. And all Fletcher put on was a pair of gym shorts.

He led her down the curved staircase at a brisk trot, then turned toward a tiled sunroom furnished in rattan. A round table was set for two, and Nona began carrying in dishes.

Fletcher held Adair's chair for her while she studied the bowl of purplish paste in front of her. "That's *poi*," he said, sitting across from her. With relish, he dipped his fingers right in the bowl and scooped up a mouthful. Adair watched, wide-eyed.

Nona put a steaming platter in front of them, and Fletcher reached over to transfer a hot bundle to his plate. He gingerly peeled away what looked like a leaf wrapping, then began eating the contents with his fingers again. Adair looked at the fork sitting beside his plate.

"*Lau lau*," he explained, nodding at the second bundle on the platter. "Try it." Adair removed it to her plate by hand. While waiting for it to cool, she stuck her fingers in the bowl and tentatively licked *poi* off them. It was smooth and bland.

"Like this," Fletcher said, showing her how to curve her first two fingers into a scoop. He reached over the table to position her fingers correctly, and she giggled. Fletcher smiled back at her, looking happier than she had ever seen him.

The *lau lau* was a spicy pork-potato combination which went well with the tamer *poi*. Adair also tried the baked breadfruit and the *lomi* salmon (which was raw, she discovered), but her courage failed at the limpets. It was all strange, new fare which she would never have touched in other circumstances, but with nearly naked Fletcher sitting across from her eating with his fingers, it was not only appropriate, but good.

When they were done, Fletcher sat back with a blissful sigh. "You just can't get that on the mainland," he declared. "First time I went stateside—" He was interrupted by the sound of the front doorbell. "Didn't the gate close behind us?" he asked Adair as he scooted his chair toward the wall. She was trying to remember if it had when he flipped the intercom switch on the wall.

They listened while Nona answered the door: "What?"

A male voice replied, "Excuse me, ma'am, but I understand that Fletcher Streiker maintains a home in this area. Could you direct me? It's very important that I see him." Adair frowned. *I know that voice.*

Nona's reply was swift and decisive: "*Lolo!* Go! *Wikiwiki!*"

"He'd want to see me," the man insisted, a shade weaker.

"What's wrong?" Fletcher asked Adair.

"Do you recognize that voice?" she asked.

"No," Fletcher shook his head. "Do you?"

"I . . . don't know," she hesitated. Meanwhile, Nona drove the anonymous caller away with a fierce barrage of pidgin. "Too late now," Adair added.

"He'll show up again," Fletcher said confidently, clicking off the intercom. "Some of my would-be visitors are quite persistent, even though nobody knows for sure that I live here." He glanced up at a wall clock as he wiped his hands on a damp napkin. "I've got to call Chuck before we go to the funeral."

He reached over to pick up a cellular phone from a glass-topped table. While he dialed, Adair gazed outside at a coconut grove reaching far overhead. She could not shake the persistent expectation that a movie crew would certainly appear on the lawn at any moment.

"Bring me up to date, Chuck," Fletcher said, leaning back in his chair.

"There's not much to tell you. I've made zero progress since we last talked," Charles said in exasperation. By leaning forward slightly, Adair could just hear him. When Fletcher glanced up and saw her listening, he tilted the phone away from his ear for her. "After that article hit the paper yesterday, vultures have been hanging all over every move I make. I'm at a standstill until I can get them off my back," Whinnet told him.

"Who are they?" Fletcher asked.

"The old cadre of movers and shakers, plus every new hotshot out to make a fast buck. They smell blood and they won't be happy till they get some," Charles said testily.

"'Zat right?" muttered Fletcher. He gazed out over the landscaped hillside beyond the house, thinking.

"I can put Harle to work," Chuck offered somewhat chillingly.

"I can only see that stirring up more media interest," Fletcher vetoed. "Besides which, I told Harle to pick up my personal cargo and take it to Paia on Maui—he's to wait there until Adair and I meet him. You might check and see that he got off okay. As for the old boys, make sure Yvonne leaks that I'm in Honolulu for my mother's funeral."

"If you say so. What's this personal cargo?" Whinnet asked.

"Harle knows," Fletcher replied. "I'll get back with you."

"Okay, good," Chuck said, and Fletcher hung up.

"When did you talk to Harle?" Adair asked.

Fletcher glanced up with a slightly guilty look. "Last

night on the plane, when you were asleep. I didn't see any need to wake you."

"Just curious," she assured him. "But why did you want Yvonne to leak that you're in Honolulu? What are you going to do?"

"Well, I'm going to try to divert the old boys from messing with my business," he said vaguely. "Meanwhile, Harle is bringing your business to Paia. I can't waste another day before getting you acquainted with it."

"When do we go?" she asked excitedly.

"Right after the funeral," he said, smiling at her interest. "So—let's go get ready." He pushed his chair back and stood.

Nona came in and silently began clearing the table. Fletcher passed her without a word, then doubled back to sneak up on her with a kiss on the cheek. "*Mahalo nui loa*," he told her.

She was startled, then pursed her lips and shoved him away by the shoulder. Bridling a laugh, he took Adair's hand to lead her back upstairs.

In privacy of the bedroom, she broached, "Fletcher, Desirée seemed to mean it when she asked you not to come."

Taking light slacks and a native's print shirt from the freestanding wardrobe, Fletcher curled his lips in a tight smile. "Desirée knows better than to tell me what to do."

Adair came up beside him, her attention diverted by the wardrobe from which he had taken the dress she now wore. There were several others hanging up as well. As she pulled out a soft lilac muumuu, she asked, "Are these mine?" Anything in her suitcase from Dallas she now considered totally inappropriate.

"Yes. I asked Nona to have some things here for you," he replied, shaking out the pants. "That's a good

77

one," he added with a nod to the dress.

Adair donned it, finding it a little more substantial than the gauze, and as she slipped sandals on her feet, wondered, "Will Desirée be upset to see us?"

"Ah, I don't think so," he replied, deliberately casual. "Are you ready?"

"No!" she exclaimed. "I've got to put on makeup and roll my hair."

He studied her critically. "Forget it. Let's go." He insistently pulled her down the staircase after him. "Bye, Nona!" he called as they headed out the door. Adair did not hear an answer.

They climbed into the sports car (which Adair now saw to be a Porsche Carrera 2), and Fletcher took off down the long driveway. Past the gate, they intersected Tantalus Drive, the lush, curvy road that wound down from the mountain. Adair held her hair back from her face to watch the deep reaches of green pass by.

Fletcher drove into downtown Honolulu to an old stone church. Adair grew nervous on seeing the large crowd there, but Fletcher parked and nonchalantly took her hand to walk her through the milling bodies. All Adair really saw were countless cameras.

He approached the steps and looked up at the two solemn, wide-bodied ushers guarding the entrance to the church. "Do you know them?" she whispered to Fletcher.

He shook his head. "Probably goons that Desirée hired. She can be so irritating," he muttered under his breath. Fletcher looked around for a moment, then led her back through the crowd to the side yard of the church, where masses of brilliant red bougainvillaea protected the old stone walls. The shrubs were cut away around a three-foot-by-four-foot stained-glass window depicting the Good Shepherd.

Fletcher folded his hands and quietly contemplated the window until he was sure no one was watching. Then he braced himself on the lower corners of the window and shoved as hard as he could. With a groan, the window swung open on a pivot halfway up and Fletcher climbed into the opening. He stood and pulled her through, then gently leaned on the window to close it again. "We used to play hide-and-seek around here, until I got spanked for it," he whispered.

Adair covered her mouth and looked around. They were standing in an alcove, the sides of which obscured them from the few persons already in the sanctuary. The funeral director suddenly appeared from a side door and strode down the nave, instructing someone at the front: "Mrs. Shaw and her family are on their way. She wants it announced that her brother is not expected to attend today." The suits in the church followed him out to the front steps, leaving an echoing silence behind them.

Fletcher watched them go, then slid out from the alcove to the front, where his mother's casket sat open, surrounded by an array of wreaths and sprays. Fletcher leaned on the casket and looked in. Adair came to his side to quietly regard the doctored remains of his mother.

"Bye, Mom," he said softly. "I'll miss you. Tell Dad hello." Adair bit her lip, overwhelmed with guilt that he had not been able to say this to her when she could have responded. "You know," Fletcher said, resting an elbow on the casket as he looked up at his wife, "one thing about my mom: she never held a grudge. And where she is, I can't imagine her starting to now."

Adair smiled at him and he straightened, hearing some ominous clatter from the entryway. He drew her to a side door and they slipped inside. He turned to his left to unlock a door to the outside. Then they tiptoed up a wooden flight of steps to a small balcony over-looking the nave. For the time being, he was careful to stay out of sight to anyone below.

While they listened to the doleful organ music and the sounds of the seats being filled, Adair watched Fletcher. He winked at her slyly, and she remembered with a shiver his telling Chuck to let it slip that he would be here today. Did he intend to actually let himself be seen? What in the world was he thinking?

It was apparent from the sudden hush when Desirée and her family entered. They were seated, and after a moment of impressive silence, the minister got up to make his remarks. "Friends and family, let us not talk about death. What is death but merely another plane of life? And we are gathered here to celebrate life—the life of a woman who was not afraid of new challenges and adventures. A woman of strength and independence, a woman of—yes, substance, my friends, who knew how to wring every drop out of life and make it endure. We can still consider her as much with us today as she ever was."

"That's not her minister," Fletcher whispered, edging around the corner to look down. "Who is this guy? Sounds like he didn't even know her."

"Pooh!" a woman's voice said in a loud whisper, evidently in response to the minister's comments. He did not miss a beat in his eulogy, choosing to treat the interruption as a cough.

Fletcher peered curiously down over the balustrade. Then he broke into a grin: "Aunt Margot!" he whispered to Adair. "Feisty old broad. I love her." Adair peeked down at the tall Anglo woman in a severe blue suit.

The minister continued, "Oona left the world gifts of love in her children, especially her wonderful daughter Desirée Streiker Shaw, her only child to be with her at the time of her passing. And in this uncertain day and age, it is a comfort to know that one's familial love still matters more than business pursuits, and can never be auctioned off as merely monetary concerns can be—"

"Harumph!" Aunt Margot cleared her throat disdainfully.

Several people turned to stare at her and the minister glanced at her. But he was on a roll: "—bankrupted, ended, swept into obscurity. Oh, the vanity of man to believe that his material resources will carry him through the tides of life! In the end, he finds himself alienated from his loved ones, unable to share their sorrows or their comfort. The seduction of wealth, my friends, is that it builds walls which isolate but cannot protect!"

"Crackpot!" Aunt Margot muttered indignantly, loud enough for Adair and Fletcher to hear. The woman next to her cringed. "What does he know about Fletcher, anyway? What kind of a preacher is that?" Margot demanded of the woman on her other side.

He was a controlling one, if nothing else. Eye contact with an usher was all that was required to have Aunt Margot forcibly assisted from her seat. As she was being escorted to the door, Fletcher leaned on the balustrade above them. "Bless you, Auntie. You never could abide a hypocrite," he said in a voice clear enough for hard-of-hearing Margot to understand at once.

Gasping in one breath, the mourners looked up at Fletcher on the balcony. It took all of Adair's courage to stand beside him in view of their eyes and not shrink back against the door.

Fletcher did not wait for them to revive from their shocked motionlessness. "I'll call you, Aunt Margot!" he promised, then grabbed Adair's hand to tear down the steps and out the back door as bedlam ensued behind them.

# 6

"**W**hat are you doing?" Adair gasped.

"Running," Fletcher responded as they dashed to his car in the church's parking lot. They jumped in and Fletcher peeled out of the lot. Behind them, mourners rushed out of the church smack-dab into a confused crowd of Streiker-spotters waiting with loaded cameras. Glancing in his rear-view mirror with a tight smile, he asked, "Do you suppose they figured out it was me?"

Adair fastened her seat belt and gathered up her wind-whipped hair. "Fletcher, I know you must have a good reason for that. I wish I knew what it was."

"I'm sorry, Adair," he chuckled, "I've been by myself for so long that I tend to improvise without a thought as to explaining it to anyone." He merged into freeway traffic en route to the airport.

"Margot had him pegged," he stated. "Mother would've been incensed by that guy using her funeral service as an opportunity to attack me. But hauling him up short wasn't my main intent. Just a side benefit." He checked his rear-view mirror warily.

"You know what a killdeer is, Adair? The bird?" he asked. She shrugged slightly. "It's a little brown bird that builds its nest right on the ground. That would seem to be a stupid thing to do; but when predators get too close to her nest, the mama killdeer will lure them away by pretending to be wounded. It's actually a very effective defense. I hope I can do half as well."

Adair eyed him and he explained, "I intend to lure the predators away from the business that's most important to me."

"By exposing yourself?" she asked in dismay. "Fletcher, what happens if they catch you?"

"I'll fly away," he said, turning down a long drive on the outskirts of Honolulu International. He parked the car next to a weathered aluminum maintenance building, then got out and stuck his head in the garage's open doors.

A swarthy young mechanic in coveralls glanced up, then broke into a wide grin. "Bossman! Whatcha here for? Name it. If it's not ready to fly, then you just serve me up *kalua* at yer next luau."

Tossing him the keys to the sports car, Fletcher said, "Okay, how about the Blackbird?"

"Hey, hey, hey!" the mechanic chortled in superiority, pointing at him. "Thought you'd fake me out, huh? Blackbird's spit-shined and on deck!" He swung his finger out to a black helicopter sitting on a pad.

"Spud, you're one *da kine brah*," Fletcher admitted. Pulling Adair forward, he added, "Adair, Spud. If ever I'm not around, Spud can get you wherever you need to go."

The mechanic wore the responsibility like a crown.

"Anywhere in the world, Mrs. Bossman," he said cockily.

Satisfied, Fletcher picked up a telephone and dialed. "Leo," he said, "two things: Margot Penner—ah, she's probably staying at the Pagoda Hotel—pick up her hotel bill and send a car to drive her wherever she wants to go while she's on the island. Make sure he takes her to Wo Fat on me. Um? No, she'll know who it's from and why.

"Second: Find out who the minister is who conducted my mother's funeral today. I want to know everything about him, including whether he has ties to anyone in Dallas. . . . No, don't do anything but find out about him. I'll call back later. Oh—did Harle make it to Paia? Good. Adair and I are on our way." He hung up and took Adair's arm, nodding to Spud as he donned aviator shades on their way out.

They boarded the helicopter and Fletcher checked over the instrument panel, then started the engine. When they had put on their headsets, Adair asked, "Are you overreacting just a little?"

His head came up in surprise. "Overreacting?"

"Checking out the minister just because he was preaching against money. Is that a little . . . paranoid?" she asked delicately.

Fletcher's chin came up slightly. The sunglasses gave his face the ominous air of a drug lord. "Margot understood what he was getting at. I just want to find out what his problem is, that's all," he replied.

She nodded, but inwardly she was uneasy. All this talk about predators and checking people out made her worry that Fletcher might harbor some Howard Hughesian tendencies after all.

He studied her an instant before lifting off, and something about his tense expression told her he guessed what she was thinking. As the helicopter rose over

Honolulu heading east, she asked, "What is Harle carrying that you wanted me to take care of?"

"I'll explain that to you when we see him," Fletcher said, and she nodded.

Adair felt a ripple under her seat. "What was that?" she said automatically. Fletcher glanced at her and shook his head slightly.

They left Oahu behind, and Adair watched the helicopter's shadow glide across the waters of Kaiwi Channel. It was smooth sailing for a while, then she noticed uneasily that they were getting closer and closer to the choppy water below. Fletcher suddenly began scanning gauges in alarm. He reached over and tapped one, flipped a switch, then tapped again.

"What's wrong?" she asked.

"The column is balking," he said, and Adair watched it shudder in his grip. "I'm losing lift," he added, tapping the gauge again. Adair clutched the seat as the chopper began bucking. She stared at the rolling sea beneath them.

"Hang on—I'm going to try for Molokai," he said tensely, grasping the column with both hands. Adair looked ahead at dry, red, ragged cliffs rising abruptly out of the water.

With the helicopter pitching like a possessed rocking horse, Fletcher aimed as best he could for a narrow valley between two jutting cliffs. He had little hovering ability left, so when the land finally did stretch beneath them, it was all he could do to set the helicopter down without crashing. The ground rushed up and the chopper landed with a bone-jarring thud.

Adair was thrown back in her seat, but Fletcher fell sideways against the door. After the shudders of the landing had settled, it took her a minute to clear her head and unfasten her seat belt. When she looked across to Fletcher, she saw him slowly raise up, reaching for the radio. Blood streamed down his face. "Fletcher!" she cried, grabbing at him.

He put the radio to his mouth. "This is Blackbird," he gasped, "we've hit the northwest shore of Molokai. Hurry. . . ."

He let the radio drop and it crackled, "Roger, Blackbird; on our way."

Adair fell out of her side of the helicopter. As she hit the ground, she saw the row of bullet holes which had pierced the body just under her seat. She stared at them momentarily, then ran around the chopper to wrench open Fletcher's door and unstrap his seat belt. He leaned on her so she could drag him away from the helicopter.

He collapsed on the hot red dirt and Adair sank beside him to shield his face from the sun. "When Spud comes, he's to take you straight to Paia," Fletcher whispered with effort.

"No! I'm staying with you!" Adair insisted.

Fletcher almost sat up in the intensity of his reaction. "Adair—you *must* meet Harle. It's the most important thing I'll ever ask of you! If you love me, *please* go! Everything hinges on it. . . ." The strain overcame him and he lapsed unconscious in her lap.

Adair held him, shivering, and wiped blood from the gash on his forehead. In a few moments she heard the sound of a helicopter approaching; looking up, she watched it advance across the bay.

The chopper hovered a moment above them, then landed about thirty feet away in the narrow gorge. Adair ducked her head and shielded Fletcher's face from being sandblasted.

Spud hopped out of the helicopter and ran forward. "What happened?"

"We were hit by strafing!" she shouted, pointing to the side of the craft. "Fletcher had to land here. He's hurt!"

Spud started to hoist him up. "Don't worry now, Bosslady; we'll get him taken care of."

Adair agreed, helping to lift him. Then she felt prompted by duty to inform Spud, "Fletcher had said—that when you came you were to take me straight to Paia. We were supposed to meet Harle there, who had something important for me."

Spud froze. "He told you that?"

"Yes," Adair said, nodding uneasily, "right before he passed out."

"That's what we gotta do then," Spud said, releasing Fletcher's limp form back down to the ground. "Go get in my chopper."

"But Fletcher needs help!" she insisted, pained. "Whatever it is can't be more important than helping him!"

"That's not for me to judge, Bosslady. I'll radio another unit to come pick him up, but the first thing I got to do is what he ordered. I'm *pau* if I don't." He broke Adair's grip on Fletcher's arm and dragged her to his helicopter.

"But—but—," Adair stammered helplessly, looking back at her husband on the sand.

"Get in, Mrs. Streiker," he shouted over the rotors, forcing her into the seat and strapping her in. Another moment later he had lifted off. As he promised, he radioed back the situation. Adair twisted in her seat to watch the disabled black helicopter with Fletcher sprawled nearby fade from view.

Almost immediately after passing over Molokai they came upon another island, and Adair gazed down at stark cliffs and profuse vegetation, cloud-topped mountains and a serpentine highway. Spud flew right past an airfield as he followed the highway eastward. He hovered, looking for a suitable spot, then landed out of sight of the highway in a green pasture.

He cut the rotors and came around to help Adair out. "We walk to the town. This way." He gestured and Adair followed with an aching heart. What business could Harle possibly bring that would be more important than Fletcher's life?

They came to a primitive, pitted road which Spud followed up to a very small town. Adair spotted buildings, and paused in wonder. They were old, brightly painted wooden false fronts that looked like something left over from a sixties musical-western. There were artworks and crafts prominently displayed down the little street, and a handful of tourists perusing them.

Spud stopped to open a wooden screen door. "This is one of Bossman's meeting places. Let's check here." Adair entered behind him and jumped as the screen door slammed shut after her. She hazily took in the Formica bar with stools pulled up to it, the lazily turning overhead fan, the bamboo partition which separated the front area from the back. Without being quite aware of doing so, she slid onto a bar stool.

"I'm gonna look in back," Spud muttered in her ear, and disappeared. So Adair sat blankly all by herself.

A friendly native barkeep came up to lean on the bar in front of her. "What you have, *nani?*"

Adair looked at him. "I don't have any money," she said weakly.

"If you sit there and let me look at you, I give you one on the house," he offered.

"I'm . . . looking for someone. Do you know Harle Kellum?" she asked in a low voice.

"What, dat da kine *pupule* dat bus' you up ifa you

cockaroach fum dah makule guys? Nah, never see him," the barkeep explained with a big grin.

"What . . . ?" Adair asked faintly, having understood nothing but the last three words.

"Thanks, Cap'n. She'll join us in the back," said an ironic voice at her side.

Adair turned. "Harle!" she choked out, grasping him. "Fletcher's been hurt! We crashed on Molokai—"

Harle quickly hushed her. "I know. I heard. You did the right thing. Come on back." He gestured her to follow him to the rear of the restaurant, behind the bamboo screen.

Adair sat at the table he indicated in the corner. The room was otherwise empty. "What's all this about, Harle?" she asked anxiously.

"Adair, allow me to introduce Daniel," he said, extending a hand.

For the first time she saw the little boy sitting across the table from her. He was a very slight four-year-old with black hair and large brown eyes. He silently regarded her as he clutched a tattered baby blanket and a shabby stuffed bunny to his face.

"Hello," Adair said, smiling sweetly. He did not reply. Adair turned back to Harle, waiting for an answer to her question.

"Adair," Harle added softly, "this is Daniel Streiker."

"Oh!" Adair said, returning her attention to the little boy. "Is he related to Fletcher?"

"Yes," Harle said slowly. "This is his son."

"Oh!" Adair repeated. "Well, I shouldn't be surprised, as much as Fletcher loves children, but why didn't he tell me he had adopted a child?"

"Adair, look at him and tell me if you think he's adopted," Harle quietly demanded.

Gazing at the stoic little face across the table, Adair

gradually apprehended the fact: *This is his son. Fletcher has a son.* "Harle, I . . . don't understand," she whispered. "Fletcher told me he's never been married."

"He hasn't," Harle said, dropping into the chair between them. "I don't know all the details, but I'll tell you what I do know. Obviously, Fletch was involved in a serious relationship. For reasons I don't know, the woman wouldn't marry him. After Daniel was born, she tried to keep Fletch from seeing him—sometimes she went to pretty extreme lengths to hide him from him.

"About a year ago, Fletch found out where they were staying after she had disappeared for a couple of months. He was on his way to see her when she took off with the boy in her car. It was a nasty night; she was sailing along pretty fast—well, she ran off the road into a tree. She was killed instantly. Daniel was not hurt, except for being trapped in the car with her for several hours. By the time help got to him . . . anyhow, he hasn't said a word since." Harle glanced across at the child; Adair's eyes had not left Daniel's face while Harle spoke.

"Then . . . this—this business that Fletcher had for me—that was so important to him—," Adair stammered.

"This is Daniel," Harle repeated quietly. "Adair, you and I are the only two people from Dallas who even know about this kid. Fletch's been keen on protecting him, sending him to the best trauma specialists in the world. Nothing's helped. They finally said the only thing that's likely to help him is a long, stable family relationship."

"Then," Adair said in a slow monotone, "he married me to be a surrogate mother to his son. My big job is to be a baby-sitter."

Harle sat back. "However you look at it, the fact is that this kid is the most important thing in the world to Fletch right now. He's ditching his company just to make time for him, and that's probably going to cost him more money than you could count in your lifetime. If you love Fletch as much as you say you do, maybe you'll share some of that concern."

Adair turned to Harle with shallow, angry breathing. "He should have told me about this. It was not right to keep it a secret from me."

His shoulders came up a fraction of an inch. "Probably. There are probably some heavy-duty reasons he didn't. Right now, that's not the main issue. The big question is, what are you going to do about it?"

Adair's mouth hung slack as she looked back at the child. He was watching her with large, expressionless eyes, as one would regard a mildly interesting alien whose appearance ranked just below face-washing in excitement. Clearly, he was not hanging with suspense on her decision. She was not even sure that he understood what was going on. But something in those vacuous eyes touched her. Their emptiness cried out to her. How could any child of Fletcher's be so emotionally impoverished?

She drooped. "What does he want me to do?" she asked dully.

"This accident has changed up things considerably. For now, I'm going to take you and Daniel to a farm owned by some friends of Fletch's. You two need to stay there until I get him to you," Harle said.

"All right," she nodded. *Hurt or not, you've got a lot of fast talking to do when I see you, Mister,* she mentally telegraphed to her husband.

Harle stood and picked up Daniel, who allowed himself to be carried but held on to his blankie and bunny. Adair followed them out the back door to a Jeep. "Spud—," she mentioned, turning.

"He's probably back on Molokai right now," Harle said. He strapped Daniel in the back seat of the Jeep beside a zippered nylon bag. Adair sat up front, and Harle started the engine.

He drove down a narrow, rutted road into the up-country. They passed fields of imposing sugar cane, which gave way to rolling pasture. Adair stared at horses grazing behind wooden fences. Harle turned past one of these corrals and pulled up to a weathered red frame house with white trim.

Unbuckling Daniel from his seat, he carried the boy and his bag up steps and through a large front porch to a screen door. Adair followed, shying away from the aggressive rooster-in-command who came over to investigate the intruders.

Harle banged on the screen door. "Hello? Anybody home?"

"Yeah?" A woman of Oriental-Polynesian ancestry came to the door, wiping her hands on the apron she wore over her faded work dress. She looked to be a strong and healthy fifty, a no-nonsense farm wife.

"Mrs. Lokomaikai, I'm Harle Kellum, an employee of Mr. Streiker. Adair and Daniel here belong to him. Could they stay with you until he comes for them?" Harle asked straightforwardly.

She barely glanced at the two before jerking her head toward the house. "Come on in, but I'm very busy. I can't see after you."

"Thanks, Mrs. Lokomaikai. All they need is a place to stay. I'll be in touch," Harle nodded. He set Daniel down and gave Adair his bag. She forlornly watched Harle trot back to the Jeep. Daniel looked straight ahead with the disinterest of a much-shuffled traveler.

"This way," their hostess said curtly, moving down a short hallway. She opened the door into a plain little room with a dresser and two small beds. "You sleep here," she said. "Now, I am very busy. Go anywhere you want but out into the fields—we are harvesting the onions. You must watch the child because I can't do it."

With that, she turned to stride back down the hall. A few moments later, Adair heard a screen door slam, and caught a glimpse out the window of the woman leaving with a basket under arm.

"Well." Adair turned to look at Daniel. He climbed up on one bed and sat swinging his feet. Studiously, he rearranged blankie and bunny under his chin. Then he sat swinging his feet and staring at the wall.

Hesitantly, Adair sat down on the bed beside him. "Well, Daniel, looks like it's you and me. Would you . . . like to play a game?" she asked tentatively. She knew he would not answer her and she didn't know any games to play, but she didn't know what else to say.

As Daniel gazed ahead blankly, a wave of irritation swept over her. Fletcher could pay an army of full-time nannies to care for his son, and any one of them would adore this beautiful, fragile child. So why her? And the fact that he had been less than forthright about it rankled her. She felt like she had been deceived.

She sighed a deep, disgusted sigh, then looked down at the boy's skinny brown legs swinging back and forth. He wore shorts and no shoes. Adair shook her head at the ragged state of the billionaire's son, and wondered if he even *had* any shoes. She leaned over to unzip his bag and look through it: several changes of clothes, sandals, underwear, a toothbrush, a little blue cup, and a wooden box.

Curious, Adair took out the box to look it over. It was so beat up that the painted design had almost worn off. It had rounded corners and a winding mechanism at the bottom, like a music box. But it would not open.

Daniel reached over and removed his property from her hands. He carefully wrapped it up in his blankie and held it to his chest. "I'm sorry. I didn't mean to pry," Adair said. "Will you show me how it works?"

For a few minutes he did nothing but continue to swing his legs. Then he paused, unwrapped his box, and replaced it in his bag. Pointedly, he buried it under the clothes. That done, he lay down on the bed, staring at the wall.

"You're tired. Go ahead and rest," Adair said encouragingly. She reached over to gingerly stroke his greasy black hair, wondering when he'd had his last bath.

Ignoring her touch, he unfurled his blanket, searching along the edge until he found a frayed corner. This he twisted to a sufficient point and stuck in his mouth. Then he closed his eyes. His point was clear: *Go away.*

Adair patted him gently on his scrawny back and got up from the bed. She left the room, quietly shutting the door behind her. Then she found her way to the kitchen to see if there might be anything to eat.

The room looked much like a farmhouse kitchen anywhere would look, with a rustic wood floor and papered walls. Adair was a little surprised and greatly relieved to find a sink with running water, a stove, and a refrigerator. There was an assortment of clutter, home-baked bread, and fresh fruit lying around; after some deliberation Adair settled on the papaya.

She ate several slices, then with a pang of conscience remembered Daniel. Who knows when he'd eaten last? Adair arranged the rest of the fruit on a plate and took it with her to the bedroom. She opened the door quietly, in case he was already asleep. "Daniel, I have some—"

He wasn't there.

# 7

**A**dair stared blankly into the room. The bed where he had been lying was barely mussed. His nylon bag still sat on the floor. "Daniel?" She came in and set the plate on the bed to look under it and the other bed as well. "Daniel?" She looked in the small closet, then went back out into the hall. "Daniel!"

She looked in every room off the hall while her heartbeat escalated. He was not in the house.

Adair ran out the back kitchen door and gazed fearfully toward the fields, where a tractor lumbered and sturdy hands toiled. "Daniel!" she called, not too loudly lest they hear her way out there. The woman had firmly told Adair to look after him, so in her runaway imagination she saw him falling under the tractor or wandering lost through the sugar cane.

She turned to scan all around—the horse barn and corral on one hand, a tomato patch on the other—and at the edge of the chicken coop, leaning on the wire looking in, was Daniel.

Adair slumped in relief and ran to him. "You scared me!" she exclaimed, picking him up so he could have a better view of the laying hens. "I got scared when I couldn't find you!"

Of course, he said nothing; he merely grasped bunny and blankie in one little hand so he could hold on to the fence with the other. Adair held him in her arms, feeling the bones under his skin. In spite of the fact that he smelled strongly, she squeezed him close. "I wouldn't want to lose you when Daddy's about to come," she murmured.

He went rigid, with a little shudder, and clung to the fence with both hands to prevent being carried into the house. Surprised at the strength that almost hauled him out of her arms, she hastily added, "Well . . . not right away. He won't be coming right away. Let's stay here and look at the chickens. Which one do you like?"

She focused on the chickens, where he gazed. They were mostly red and brown, but there was one scrappy, speckled rooster that harassed the hens and foraged importantly for bugs. He did not back down for anything but the dominant rooster, a great big red one.

"I like the spotted one. See?" she pointed. "He likes to be different. He doesn't care what the others think. Look, he found something! He's so proud of himself. What's he eating?"

Daniel watched the speckled rooster and gradually relaxed. "Are you hungry, Daniel? I found some papaya in the kitchen. Would you like something to eat?" she asked softly.

After a moment Daniel let go of the fence, signaling his willingness to be taken inside. Adair carried him in—he was not very heavy—and sat him at the wooden table in the kitchen.

"Let me go get the plate. I left it in the bedroom. Don't move," she added warily before darting back for the plate.

When she returned seconds later he was still at the table. Adair set the papaya in front of him and asked, "Would you like some milk?" He said nothing, but laid bunny and blankie on the table to start in greedily on the fruit.

Too late Adair saw how dirty his hands were. "Oh, dear—you're—oh, well." She didn't see any peaceable way of separating him from his meal to wash his hands, so she just let him eat.

She found a glass in the cupboard and poured him some milk. He ate all the papaya, drained the glass of milk, then hopped down from the table and out of the kitchen with startling quickness, bunny and blankie in tow. Adair leapt after him in time to see him go into the bathroom and shut the door.

She hovered outside the door, listening, until she heard the toilet flush and the door opened. He started to come out but Adair turned him firmly by the shoulders back to the sink. "Look, Daniel! We're going to wash our hands! Oh, boy! Now, let's put your things right here so they won't get wet." She patted the toilet-tank top. "They'll wait right here for you. Good," she said as he hesitantly laid his treasures close by.

He could not reach the faucet, so she held him up to the lavatory to soap up his little hands in hers. She knuckled on the water to rinse and reached for a bath towel to dry. It was such a big towel she pretended it to be an alligator gobbling up his hands: "GARUMPH! Umm, yummy, yummy!" she growled. His only reaction was to blink.

They came out of the bathroom and Adair hesitated, looking for something to do. But Daniel went right back to the bedroom and climbed onto the bed. He sat, swinging his legs.

Adair slowly sat on the bed opposite and watched him. He carefully gathered up the blankie in a compact bundle and tucked it with bunny into his chest, just under his chin. Adair looked out the window toward the horse barn. "They have horses, Daniel. Would you like to go look at the horses?" she asked.

He did nothing for a few seconds. Then as if it were his own idea, he slid down from the bed and went out toward the corral. Adair followed. Holding open the screen door, she offered her hand to him. He ignored the gesture, gathering his things up tightly under his chin.

They walked down from the porch to the wooden fence surrounding the dirt pen. There were two horses, a black and a sorrel, which stood languidly foraging for what sparse tufts of grass they had not already plucked up. Adair lifted Daniel to stand on the lower plank of the fence so that he could see better.

"Aren't they pretty horses?!" she remarked. It was getting tiresome talking to someone who never responded. "Maybe they'll let us ride them. Would you like to ride one, Daniel?" He blinked at the horses. After a few minutes he had seen enough of them, and climbed down from the fence. He went back to the bedroom to sit on the bed and swing his legs.

Thus the afternoon hours crawled by with excruciating slowness. Adair had never been much interested in children and had no notion of what to do with one, especially in a strange house on another planet. Daniel gave her no clues. As a matter of fact, he showed so little cognizance of anything that she began to wonder if he were mentally impaired. He passed the entire afternoon staring into space, locked away in his own mind.

Adair made several more attempts to draw his interest to something or the other, but she was hopelessly hampered by the lack of toys and Daniel's own refusal to be interested. Once, he reached down into his bag and withdrew the small wooden box. Too eagerly, Adair sat beside him. "Oh, show me your box, Daniel! Show me what's in it!" He held his box a moment, then secreted it once again in the bottom of his bag.

Their hostess (Adair could not remember how to pronounce her name) did not return to the house until time to start preparing dinner; and when she did, she gave no notice at all to her guests. That did not much help Adair's state of mind.

She began to worry as evening approached without any word from Fletcher. He must have been hurt pretty badly. Daniel's reaction to the mere suggestion that his father would be coming was alarming as well. Adair wondered what had caused Daniel to be so frightened of him. Then she considered that if his mother had spent every waking moment running from Fletcher, Daniel might as well be terrified of the prospect of seeing him. What had Fletcher done to make her run?

It was a relief to smell supper cooking. Adair left Daniel to himself on his bed and entered the kitchen. "Can I help you?" she asked with a smile.

Mrs. L hardly glanced up at her. "No. You just watch the child and keep him out of trouble. That's all you need to do."

Adair drooped. "Have you heard anything from Fletcher yet?"

"No," the woman answered. "You'll know when we do." She dropped the ladle from the pot she was stirring and went out to call the men to dinner with a loud yell.

As she came back in, allowing the kitchen screen door to slam behind her, Adair asked tightly, "May Daniel and I eat with you?" She no longer knew what to assume.

The woman looked at her in surprise. "Of course," she said, insulted that Adair should have to ask. So Adair went out to fetch Daniel from the bedroom.

She held him back out of the way while four tired, sweaty men lumbered in, washed up, and took their places around the kitchen table. When they were all seated there remained two empty seats on the far end, so Adair put Daniel in one chair and took the other for herself. Gripping an oversized spoon in his fist, he began eating as soon as Mrs. L put a bowl in front of him.

Adair was encouraged when one man, brown-skinned and gray-haired, obviously the patriarch of the family, smiled at her and said, "Hello." She beamed at him and returned his greeting. She had started to thank him for his hospitality when another man began talking and from that point on, Adair and Daniel were invisible.

Dinner was a thick vegetable stew, homemade bread, and several side dishes of something like cabbage and some kind of beans. The family was engrossed in conversation about the wholesale distributor of the onions they were harvesting—the company had made unfulfilled promises and untimely payments. It was a very serious situation because this distributor had forced out its only viable competitor and now held all the cards.

Adair listened quietly, having nothing to add until it dawned on her to ask, "Have you discussed this with Fletcher? Surely he can do something."

Her comment brought abrupt silence. Then one man informed her, "This wholesaler is one of his companies—used to be, until he sold it. He sold us out."

Red-faced, Adair stared down at her plate. Suddenly there was a loud knocking on the front screen door. Adair jumped up and Daniel scrambled under the table.

Harle was standing outside the front door. Adair ran to throw open the door in relief. "Harle! Thank goodness!" she exclaimed. "How's Fletcher?"

He stood back on the porch squinting at her. Then he made his decision. "Okay, Adair. You're a big girl; I'm going to tell you the truth." Adair's stomach knotted up. He said, "By the time they got a medic to Molokai Fletch was gone. We don't know what happened to him, but we believe he didn't walk off on his own."

"Oh, Harle. . . ." She closed her eyes and leaned against the door frame.

"We're looking for him, Adair. We've got the world's quietest manhunt going on. You and Daniel are safest staying right here. Okay?" he asked, and she nodded limply. "I'll keep you informed," he said, moving off toward his Jeep.

"Harle," she said suddenly, "he . . . felt like the minister who conducted his mother's service today had a grudge against him. Fletcher asked somebody to check him out."

"I know about that," he said, swinging up into the seat.

"Harle," she said, and he paused while she came up to the Jeep. She was deeply reluctant to let him go. He was one familiar, trusted face in a harrowing situation. Casting a glance over her shoulder, she told him, "This family—what's their name again?"

"Lokomaikai," Harle said clearly.

"They've been having trouble with the distributor that Fletcher used to own. Can you, uh, ask Charles Whinnet to check into it, to see if the distributor can't be made to live up to their agreement?" she asked.

"Sure," he said as he started up the engine. "Hang tight, Adair. You and Daniel."

"Sure," she sighed as his Jeep lurched away.

Adair dismally returned to the kitchen, wondering what, if anything, she should tell the family about Fletcher's disappearance. But no one expressed the slightest interest in what Harle had to say.

After dinner the family gathered in one room to watch television and relax until an early bedtime. Daniel peeked into the gathering room, then shied away to go sit on his bed and kick his legs. Adair decided it was a good time to take advantage of the bathroom while no one was using it, so she began running water in the tub. While it filled, she fetched Daniel from the bed. "Bath time, Daniel," she declared.

He was less than interested, and made a halfhearted effort at escape, but Adair held him firmly to peel his clothes off him. Her heart throbbed painfully at the sight of the skinny little body, and she was momentarily furious with Fletcher at the neglected state of his own son.

After disengaging him from blankie and bunny, Adair lifted him into the tub and started scrubbing him down. He took it manfully, bony shoulders hunched and eyes squeezed shut against the soap.

When she was done with the washing part, Adair looked around in vain for bath toys. Then she left him in the tub to retrieve his blue cup and toothbrush from his bag. The cup he accepted for a toy, and Adair showed him how to trap air under the washcloth to make bubbles.

He played contentedly for a while, experimenting with dragging the air-laden cloth underwater and squeezing bubbles from it. Then someone else desired to use the bathroom, so she hurriedly lifted him out, dried him off, and coaxed him to brush his teeth.

As she carried Daniel out wrapped in the towel, the man waiting outside looked in. "Don't leave dirty clothes on the floor," he chastised. "Ow-ee, look at that tub!" he said in disgust.

Adair glanced at the grimy bathtub ring as she swept up the clothes from the floor. "I'll be right back to clean it up," she promised.

She carried Daniel into the bedroom and rubbed him thoroughly, then put underpants on him and tucked him in bed. "Goodnight, Daniel," she said, kissing him on the forehead. She felt so much better to see him washed and fed. He twisted the blankie corner and put it in his mouth, rolling onto his side. Before she stepped out to clean the tub, she whispered, "I'll be right back. Don't get out of bed."

When she came back into the room ten minutes later, Daniel was definitely asleep. She sank onto the other bed, then looked down at the muumuu she wore and struck her forehead. "Why didn't I think to ask Harle to bring me a suitcase?" She sighed, shaking her head. "Because all I could think about was . . . Fletcher."

Unable to bear speculating on what might have happened to him, she got up to check the bureau drawers. She found some long-tailed men's shirts and boxer shorts, so she changed into those. After checking Daniel once more and kissing his clean face, she turned out the light and climbed into the other bed.

❧

Deep into the night, a sound woke her—a tinkling, musical sound. After gradually coming awake enough to focus on it, Adair realized that Daniel must have gotten out his music box. It was playing a little calypso tune.

Adair raised up on her elbow. "Is that your music box, Daniel? Why don't you put it up for tonight, and show it to me tomorrow?" she suggested. After a few minutes he leaned over and put it back in the bag, where the sound was muffled until it ran down. "Thank you," Adair said, then rolled over and went back to sleep.

Some time later, Adair was awakened once again by the tinkling notes of the music box. She breathed a groan and sat up to ask him to put the darn thing away.

But a sudden, rude insight stopped her. This was a lonely child being tossed among strangers. Surrounded by darkness and uncertainty, he was holding on to a comforting, familiar sound. Considering how unwilling she had been to let Harle go, it was unthinkable for her to make Daniel put away his music box.

"It's a pretty tune, Daniel. You can listen to it all you want," she said quietly, lying back down. He held it next to him for several minutes, then put it back in the bag. Adair did not hear it the rest of the night.

The following morning Adair had considerable difficulty waking up. Never a willing riser, she was further exhausted by yesterday's traumas and today's responsibilities. On top of all that, an early winter storm was underway, sending sheets of lulling rain against the windows.

When at last Adair opened her eyes, she looked around lazily and rolled on her side toward Daniel's bed. As soon as she glimpsed the mussed, empty sheets she sprang up and bolted out of the bedroom to look for him.

She ran into the kitchen and halted awkwardly, still dressed in the man's shirt and shorts. The kitchen was full of the Lokomaikai family, who were watching the rain with great disgust. Adair quickly gleaned that they could not continue harvesting with the tractor in the rain, and if it didn't let up soon, they'd have to get out there and do it by hand. This sufficiently engrossed them so that no one saw her; and as Daniel was not there, she backed out quietly to look elsewhere.

She found him huddled on the front porch in his underwear. He also was watching the rain as it gained force. The large front porch, protected by an overhang, allowed ample room for four or five people to pull up chairs and look over the gently rolling pasture to Haleakala Crater. But today Daniel sat alone with his blankie, bunny, and music box while the elements roared around him, the tinkly calypso tune barely audible above the storm.

The sight broke her heart. Shivering with emotion, Adair looked on a bruised, defenseless little soul and loved him with every impulse of her being. How could she not? If anything happened to Fletcher, Daniel was all she would have left of him. At that moment she forgave Fletcher any and every transgression in not telling her about him.

The music box faltered and stopped; Daniel studiously rewound it with stubby fingers. As it began replaying the tune stronger, he tucked the blankie under his chin and gazed at the rain.

Adair listened to the music. Something about the bouncy beat reminded her of a dance she'd learned long ago, a dance about a music-box ballerina that comes to life. It had been at least fifteen years since she had done that dance, but thinking of the music brought the steps to her feet.

Adair turned her back to Daniel, who looked up. She raised her arms over her head and braced the sole of one foot against the other calf. Then, to the music, she stole one quick glance over her shoulder at him. *Is anyone watching?* the plastic ballerina asks, poised on one foot. She looked quickly over her other shoulder. *Is it safe?*

Carried away by the music, the ballerina suddenly steps off her spring and dances down from the box. She glides and pirouettes with the joy of being free. Daniel watched with slightly widened eyes. The steps came back fresh and infallible as Adair performed to music-box accompaniment for her audience of one. And at the end, as the music ran down, the ballerina must resume her stance on one foot, merely a plastic decoration.

Adair turned and made a low, perfectly executed formal bow. Daniel gaped at her, and slowly his mouth turned out in a smile. It grew until it covered half his face and made his eyes squint. He hunched his shoulders in delight, digging his fists into his lap.

Adair gasped, seeing the stark resemblance to his father's face. She burst into tears and grabbed him up for a crunching hug. After a moment of painful indecision, Daniel slipped his arms around her neck.

They hugged each other tightly while Adair wet his scrawny neck with her tears. Then a shift in the wind sent a sheet of rain under the porch overhang; Adair quickly gathered up the dropped box and bunny and carried all the treasures inside.

She took Daniel to the bedroom and dressed him. Then she showed him the music box before carefully packing it away in his bag. She scooped him up in her arms and carried him to the family room.

No one else was there right now. Adair turned on the radio to a pop-rock Hawaiian station, then extended her hands to Daniel in an invitation to dance.

He dropped blankie and bunny right on the floor to take her hands. Over the next hour they slow-danced, boogied, waltzed, and jitterbugged, not always in perfect synchronization with the music. Adair never saw the smiling faces of the Lokomaikais peeking into the room; nor did she notice when the sun came out and they left for the fields. All she saw was her flushed, happy dance partner. He was naturally graceful and rhythmic, and a quick study.

After their umpteenth dance Adair dropped breathless to the woven grass floor: "Dan'l, you wore me out! I'm pooped!" So he retrieved his blankie and bunny to sit beside her. Adair lifted him onto her lap, where he nestled down. She closed her eyes, holding Fletcher's son close to her chest.

Then her stomach growled. Adair looked toward the kitchen. "Daniel, I'm hungry! Have you had anything to eat?" He only shifted in response. Adair resolved as her next major goal to get him to talk.

She stood, taking him to the kitchen. (He was so light it just seemed natural to carry him around.) Adair put him in a chair and began nosing for brunch.

Mrs. Lokomaikai was not in the kitchen, but there was a pot of rice still on the stove, and still almost warm. Adair spooned some out in two bowls and put them on the table, one in front of Daniel. He blinked at her expectantly. "What?" she asked blankly.

With a sigh, he placed blankie and bunny beside his bowl and slid down from the chair. He scrounged in the refrigerator until he found butter. Then he climbed up on the counter to get the sugar. These he brought to the table with a certain air of impatience.

Adair laughed. "Sorry, you're going to have to start telling me what you want."

She watched as he doctored up his rice with butter

and sugar. "That looks pretty good," she admitted, sitting with him. "Pass the butter, please."

They enjoyed a pleasant, albeit nonverbal brunch, then Adair ran a hand through her hair, wondering what she looked like. She glanced out toward the Lokomaikais working far out in the fields. "I've got to take a shower," she mused.

In the family room, Adair found a picture book and sat Daniel down with it. "I have to get cleaned up, Daniel. Please don't wander off while I'm in the bathroom—I'll get scared if I come out and can't find you. If you'll sit here and look at the book while I get ready, we'll go for a walk. Okay? Please?" He noncommittally opened the book, stuffing blankie and bunny in the space between his crossed legs.

Adair set a speed record showering that morning. She toweled her hair dry and put on the boxer shorts under her muumuu, then washed out her solitary pair of panties. "I'm a billionaire's wife," she reminded herself ironically.

Opening the bathroom door, she almost fell over the small body on the floor just outside. Daniel looked up, a corner of the blankie in his mouth. "Were you waiting for me?" she asked in surprise, and he got up expectantly. "Oh, Daniel." She pressed his forehead to hers. "Let's go get our shoes."

Adair took his hand and they went to the bedroom, where she laid out her panties to dry and put on her sandals. As she dug his sandals out of his nylon bag and put them on him, she eyed his ever-present companions.

"Daniel, I don't think your bunny rabbit and your blanket want to go with us. They're afraid of getting dirty or lost. And if you have to carry them, you won't be able to carry any other interesting things we might find. Why don't you let them wait right here in your bag? They can keep your music box company." She encouragingly held the bag open for him.

Daniel rocked hesitantly, then looked at his precious bunny and blankie. He looked in the bag. Deliberately, he wadded up the blankie and placed both items in the bag. His hands were now completely free.

"Great!" Adair exclaimed, shaking him gently by the middle. He took the fingers of her right hand with both his hands, holding on tight. Adair kissed the little hands and stood up. "Let's go see what we find, Daniel."

**H**and in hand, Adair and Daniel walked up the rutted, winding road toward Paia. The recent rain had filled the ruts in the road and the air was still heavy with moisture, but the clouds had safely cleared away. The pasture they passed soon gave way to fields of sugar cane, slender giants glistening with droplets.

Shortly, they came upon one of Paia's two main streets, with its craftsmen, vendors, and tourists. Adair felt that even this small town was too public, but she spotted the ocean just beyond it, and that's what she wanted to see. So she and Daniel passed through the town and headed toward the cliffs at the edge of the world.

They had to walk quite a stretch down a two-lane road through dense tropical growth—at least a mile, Adair guessed—before they crossed Highway 36 and looked down to the sea. The wind sent huge breakers crashing up against the cliffs far below them. Profuse greenery spilled out of crevices in the cliffs as if there was just not enough room topside to hold it all.

There was no place to descend where they were, but farther down Adair spotted a beach and the sails of windsurfers. Holding tightly to Daniel's hand, she led him down a rough trail another mile or so to the white sand beach.

Daniel jettisoned his sandals and began scampering along the beach like any normal child. Adair sat to watch him play tag with the waves, and gaze up at the shorebirds, and examine the sand for hidden playthings. In this sun-drenched play, Adair saw something miraculous and earth-moving: a child without fear. A child exploring the world as a child should, under the eye of a guardian who would keep him safe from harm. It was a big compliment to be entrusted with such an awesome responsibility. Why had she never seen it that way before?

Daniel found something in the sand and brought it to her. Adair examined the striped, curled shell that covered his palm. "Oh, Daniel, how pretty! Would you like me to hold it for you while you play?" He left it with her in perfect confidence and moved off in a strange lope that she finally recognized as a four-year-old's attempt at skipping. Her heart thumped painfully.

Never ranging beyond her sight, Daniel played himself to exhaustion, then came over and dropped into her lap. He felt for his blankie, but as it was not there, accepted the shell instead. Adair rocked him contentedly.

He pointed out to the windsurfers' brightly colored sails and for one breathless moment she thought he was going to speak. But he didn't; he merely withdrew his pointing finger and curled up in the softness of her arms. In this quiet moment, life was distilled to its most elemental quality, its purest, basic form, and Adair understood the verb *to be*.

Daniel suddenly raised up and peered in her face. He dropped the shell to hold her face between his small hands. His expression was vaguely fearful and mistrustful, with a large question looming in his eyes.

"What is it?" Adair whispered in alarm. With no intention of answering, Daniel picked up his shell and climbed from her lap. He stood by the path leading up to the highway, indicating his readiness to go.

Adair slipped the little sandals back on his feet and took the hand not clutching the shell. They walked back to the highway and down the road toward Paia. Mindful of his unspoken burden, Adair swung his hand and sighed, "I'm hungry again! I suppose we could get something to eat in Paia, but I don't have any money—" Daniel suddenly let go of her hand and darted toward the jungle growth along the road. "Daniel!"

He kept running, so she ran after him. "Daniel! Stop!" Heedless, he continued threading his way through the undergrowth and she saved her breath for chasing him.

He stopped at a large tree and began climbing it. As Adair reached the foot of the tree, he dropped some bright red fruit down to her. She caught it barely and juggled it, then looked up just in time to see him chomping down on another one.

"Daniel!" she gasped. "Are you sure that's—" She broke off, watching him anxiously. From his seat on the branch, he looked down on her with a definitely superior attitude, knowing that it was not only edible, but good.

"You little monkey!" Adair cried, shaking his foot. That produced the second smile of the day. Adair bit into the fruit and found it something like a sweet apple. She ate a prodigious amount, warily watching him in the tree.

After their snack, she lifted her arms to him. "Come down now, monkey." He leaned down from the branch and she caught him under the arms. Holding him, she smiled and said, "Thank you for finding me something to eat."

He cupped her face in his little hands and kissed her right on the lips. Adair burst out laughing, then caught herself, not wanting to offend him. In all seriousness, he caressed her face like a lover. Then, ominously, that same fearful expression came over his delicate features. This time, Adair believed she understood him: *Are you going to leave me, too?*

"No," she shook her head. "I'll never leave you, Daniel. I love you." He put his head down on her shoulder and locked his arms around her neck. He clamped his legs around her middle so as to hang on even if she let go. Adair squeezed him tightly and then looked around. The dense jungle growth was equally unfamiliar in every direction.

"Daniel," she said with a chill, "I don't remember which way is the road." He let go with one arm to point behind him. Dubiously, Adair carried him through the tangle in that direction, and momentarily they broke through to the paved road. "Monkey," she muttered, and she was sure he giggled.

When they reached Paia, she stopped in Cap'n's place to see if he had heard anything from Harle today. Daniel wished to remain outside to investigate the chassis of an old Volkswagen that had been abstractly painted and set on a low cement pedestal as a work of art.

Nah, Cap'n said, he'd heard nothing from "*da kine*

*brah* Harlay. But heah—I get you an' dah *keiki* some shave ice." He opened a freezer and swirls of frigid air rolled out. Cap'n scooped out ice shavings into two paper cups and artfully drizzled them with red syrup.

Adair accepted them, grinning. "Thanks, Cap'n." She stepped outside into the warm afternoon and looked toward the painted chassis. Daniel was nowhere around it.

Anxiously, Adair scanned up and down the street. Two buildings up she saw a car stopped with the driver's door standing open. The driver was earnestly talking at Daniel, who stood just out of arm's reach, listening indecisively. Adair could not see enough of the driver to even know if it was a man or a woman.

"Daniel!" she called. He looked toward her, and seeing what she held, came running. The driver shut his door and drove off.

As Daniel reached up for his shave ice, she handed it to him and asked, "Who was that, Daniel? What did they want?" As usual, he did not answer, but he did not seem disturbed or frightened. Adair, however, began to grow wary.

❦

**B**y late afternoon they arrived back at the farmhouse. Adair felt a vague anxiety over being gone so long when she observed the activity around the house. A large truck piled high with onions sat out front, and an old station wagon behind it was being loaded.

Mrs. Lokomaikai came out wearing a bright dress and carrying a large handbag. She gestured to Adair. "We are going to Kahului to meet with the wholesaler. He called today to offer new terms. You stay as long as you need to, and don't worry with the animals. We have a neighbor coming to tend the chickens and horses."

"Everyone's going?" Adair asked anxiously. How long will you be gone?"

"It may take a few days to look at all their papers. The boys, they go to back up what we say," Mrs. Lokomaikai said sternly.

"I see," Adair murmured, watching the men pile into the cab of the truck. "Has Harle been by today? Have you heard anything about Fletcher?"

"No," the woman answered, straightening her straw hat.

The elder Mr. Lokomaikai sat behind the wheel of the station wagon. Depressed, Adair added, "I hope it goes well. Thank you for letting us stay."

Mrs. Lokomaikai waved to her before climbing into the station wagon. A few moments later they took off slowly down the uneven dirt road. Adair and Daniel stood looking after them. Clutching his shell, Daniel let go of her hand to cling to her leg instead. She understood; somebody else had just abandoned him. She felt abandoned herself. The feeling of desolation that swept over her as she watched her preoccupied hosts drive off almost swamped her—until she looked down at the black head of her charge. If she had no one else left in the world, she had Daniel. His dependence on her gave her strength.

Adair tousled the head pressed against her thigh. "We've got the whole house to ourselves, Daniel! Let's raid the refrigerator and watch TV!"

They did just that. Daniel helped her scrounge up a feast of leftovers from the kitchen. She watched him out of the corner of her eye as he laboriously spread peanut butter on a thick slice of bread and topped it with a banana.

"Umm, that looks good," she remarked, so he offered her a bite. Adair bit off the end of the banana protruding over the bread and kissed him in gratitude. He gazed at her with adoration in his eyes.

They took their feast to the gathering room and Adair turned on the television. They settled on the floor to watch a family situation comedy while they ate. The story line of the show included one scene in which the father came home from work to confront his son about a misdeed. The father entered the house, slamming the door behind him, and shouted in a deep, threatening voice, "Daddy's home!"

Daniel dropped his banana sandwich and leaped on the couch behind them. He dug down in the cushions to hide, covering his head with a crocheted pillow.

Adair quickly changed channels and went to the couch. She removed the pillow to lift a stiff, trembling little body out of hiding. When she sat on the couch to hold him on her lap, he twisted in her arms and clutched her neck for dear life. "Daniel," she began in a soft, soothing voice, "I wish I knew why you are so afraid of your daddy. I'm married to him, and I think I know him pretty well. He is a nice man. He's not going to hurt you."

She continued talking in this reassuring vein, but nothing she said eased his trembling. Finally, she dropped the subject to start reminiscing about their day. Adair talked about the sugar cane fields, and the beach, and the windsurfers. When she reminded him of the mountain apples he had found for them, Daniel stopped trembling.

Once she had talked him down from the couch, they finished eating in front of another show. Daniel laid a heavy head in her lap, his fingers searching for his blankie. He looked toward the bedroom past the dark hallway, but was too frightened of the darkness to go fetch his blankie. He stood up and pulled on her hand.

She nodded. "Time for your bath." She got up and turned off the television. The quiet darkness that settled in was somewhat scary, even to her. It was the darkness that surrounded a stranger in a strange land.

Adair swallowed her irrational fears and led Daniel by the hand to the bathroom, where she had him brush his teeth as his water was running. He would not allow her to leave him alone for even an instant, so he went with her to the bedroom to get clean underwear. She turned on every light along the way.

He had his bath and played with his shell in the tub while Adair watched. When he was done, she decided it would feel good to go to bed clean, so she started the shower. Daniel would not for the world be persuaded to sit outside in the evil hallway while she showered, so she fetched his music box to distract him while she undressed.

Soon they were both clean and ready for bed, Adair wearing the man's shirt and boxer shorts again. She tenderly tucked Daniel in with his blankie and bunny, and turned out all the lights in the house but one, for a nightlight. "We had a fun day, didn't we? Goodnight, Daniel," she whispered, settling into the other bed.

That arrangement lasted about fifteen seconds. Then Adair felt a rustle in the sheets as she was joined by Daniel, bunny, and blankie. Adair snuggled them all close. Daniel sighed, then instantly fell asleep.

Adair caressed his thick black hair as she thought back over the day to that morning. Yes, she had danced again, and her training had proved quite useful. That moment had been the icebreaker with Daniel. She could not imagine any more satisfying performance.

She looked out the open window, screened to keep out the mosquitoes, and thought about Fletcher. At some point she had completely stopped worrying about him, preoccupied as she was with her own problems. She could not visualize him being at the mercy of anyone—the more she thought about it, the more she wondered if this whole scenario weren't something he had set up just to get her acquainted with Daniel. *Well*, *it worked*, she thought wryly. After these ponderings, she hugged Daniel and drifted to sleep.

Later she woke—barely—trying to hang on to a dream she was having. She dreamed that she had wings to fly, and flew everywhere, inside houses and up to the clouds. People on the ground kept shooting at her, but her wings enabled her to dart out of the way and she was never hurt. It was a good feeling. She opened her eyes just a crack. Was that a car she heard, or was it part of the dream?

As she slowly came awake, she began to sense that something was amiss. She tightened her arm around Daniel, sleeping peacefully beside her. She lifted her head as much as she could without disturbing him to look around. What bothered her?

Her eyes focused on the hallway. It was dark. That was it—the light was out.

Adair raised up in bed. No, she was mistaken. There was the light. She peered at it. No, it looked wrong. It was too faint and flickering.

She smelled smoke. A sudden whoosh and crackle confirmed her worst, unbelievable fear. She jumped out of bed and looked down the hall at the flames growing in the kitchen. The wood-frame house was a tin-derbox waiting to explode.

Adair backed into the bedroom and shut the door. She grabbed Daniel and his bag and ran to the window. As smoke curled under the door, she unlatched the screen and kicked it out. Then she crawled out with Daniel half awake, clinging to her like seaweed.

She carried him away from the house, then sank to the ground near the sugar cane and numbly watched the flames gobble up the structure. Daniel was too ter-rified to look, but hid his face in her neck while shiv-ering spasmodically.

*What happened?* She floundered for answers. *Did I leave something on in the kitchen? Was there a short in the wiring somewhere?* At that point she remembered the sound of the car that had wakened her, and knew with-out question that it was not something she had dreamed.

Her eyes focused on two dark figures running from the back of the house. They met up in the front yard, argued briefly, and then disappeared down the road toward the upcountry without seeing her and Daniel huddled at the edge of the sugar cane field. *What?* Stunned, Adair looked down at the quivering boy cling-ing to her neck and outrage exploded within her. *Who would do this to a child? After all this little boy has been through, who would do such a horrible thing?* At that moment all the bone-dead passivity in Adair rose up with a clat-ter and put on flesh and armor. She declared war.

"Come on, Daniel," she said in a clear, firm voice as she disengaged his arms from her neck and set him on his feet. "We have to hurry to Paia to get help." She paused to make sure that the horses and chickens were not in danger. Then grasping his hand, she set off at a trot up the road and he ran along beside her, toting bunny and blankie.

They ran the entire distance to the sleepy little town. Adair zeroed in on the first building with a light inside and banged on the door: "Help! We need help! Hello!"

There were quick shuffling footsteps and the door creaked open. Adair could barely distinguish the features of the man who stood within. "We just came from the Lokomaikais' house. It's on fire! We barely got out!" she said breathlessly.

He shouted up to someone and then ran to another building. While the occupants began turning out, Adair dragged Daniel inside to a telephone. She picked it up and dialed the operator, demanding to be connected to Honolulu International Airport. She was, unfortunately, connected directly with a recording.

Adair banged around the voice-mail jail for a while, meanwhile glancing anxiously over her shoulder, until she landed a real live person on the other end of the line.

She demanded to speak with airport maintenance, and when someone there answered, she demanded Spud. "Who?" he said.

"Spud! His name's Spud!" she shouted.

"Ah, hold on." He directed a question away from the telephone. "Any you guys know Spud?" Someone indistinctly answered him, and he returned to the telephone to say, "Yeah, Spud's off duty right now."

"Give me his phone number," she ordered. "This is an emergency."

"Yeah, sure, okay, hang on," he said, and in a moment returned with the number.

Adair hung up and placed a reassuring hand on Daniel's back as he clung to her leg. When she realized he was still in his underpants, she put down the telephone to dress him in shorts and a T-shirt from his bag. That took some doing, as he would not release bunny or blankie to get dressed. But with calmness and patience she coaxed him into clothes. She withdrew farther into the darkened room as someone ran by the door on his way out, then she picked up the phone again and dialed Spud's number.

Someone answered sleepily on the first ring: "Umm?"

"Is this Spud?" she asked cautiously.

"Yes," he said, instantly alert.

"This is Adair," she said quietly. "I'm in Paia. I need you to get that jet and come get me right now."

"In the seven-twenty-seven?" he asked.

"Yes. I want you to take me straight to Dallas," she said, glancing warily at voices outside.

"Sure, Bosslady. But I can't land that jet in Paia. You'll have to get to the airport in Kahului," he said.

"Where is that?" she asked with sinking heart.

"It's only about four miles west of Paia. Take Highway Thirty-six west. You can't miss it," he said encouragingly.

"All right," she said. "But I'm going to have to walk there."

"No sweat; we'll reach the airport about the same time. Laydahs, Bosslady." He hung up and Adair laid down the receiver with a trembling hand.

Adair knelt before Daniel with a reassuring smile. Brushing the hair back from his wide eyes, she said, "We're going on a little trip, Daniel. A friend of"—she had started to say *of Fletcher's*—"of mine is coming to pick us up in a plane. It will be so much fun! But we have to walk to the airport where he can land."

So saying, she dug his sandals from his bag and put them on his feet. She herself was barefoot, but that was no concern. "Let's go," she whispered.

Taking his hand and his bag, she slipped out of the building into the street. People were running past her down the road toward the farm. Glancing that way, she could see flames lighting up the sky above the house.

Adair and Daniel trotted toward the road that had taken them to the beach earlier in the day. At this point she was extremely grateful for having made that out- ing—not only for the pleasure of getting to know Daniel, but for the lesson in island geography. She knew where Highway 36 was.

After trotting the mile to the highway, they turned west and continued on. The scenery by night was of unworldly beauty; the luxuriant roadside growth draped the cliffs in dark softness until abruptly parting at points to reveal the shimmering, endless waves crashing rhyth- mically against the lava rock, every now and then a blowhole spouting *sforzando*. The beaches glistened and the night birds called—but for the circumstances, it would have been a lovely trek.

Daniel's little legs finally gave out and Adair hoisted him to her shoulder without breaking her brisk stride. *Thank you, Madame*, she thought ironically. *It was worth a thousand dollars a day to get in shape for this.*

Those four miles to the airport proved to be a long stretch. Daniel fell asleep on her shoulder, breathing softly in her ear, and she hugged him gently. When bunny slipped from his unconscious fingers, she stopped and gracefully bent at the knees to retrieve it. She slipped it into the nylon bag and kept going. There were sharp cinders along the highway that were impossible to avoid in the darkness—before long, Adair felt as if she were walking on meat tenderizers. The accumulated jabs brought tears to her eyes but did not slow her stride.

As she approached Kahului, cars began appearing on the highway. Remembering the car she had heard, she stepped into the underbrush until they passed. She did not require a ride and was in no way going to answer any questions.

On the outskirts of the city, she saw a sign pointing to the airport off to the right. She followed that road until the airport loomed up in the darkness.

Adair paused in the parking lot, glancing around with a pounding heart. She did not know where to go from here. There was a brightly lit terminal on one hand and runway lights on the other. She watched a jumbo jet lift off into the night.

Her eyes lowered to a dark figure striding toward her. She clutched Daniel and stood her ground; whoever it was had already seen her. "Mrs. Streiker?" he asked.

"Spud?"

"Yeah." He drew up to her. "I didn't realize you had anybody with you," he remarked, eying the sleeping Daniel.

"Where is the plane?" she asked.

"This way," he said, extending his hand. As Adair began to limp along beside him, he paused to ask, "You want me to carry the kid?"

"No," she said quickly, but handed him Daniel's nylon bag.

The relief of mounting the steps to the sleek jet was overwhelming. Adair laid Daniel gently in a reclined seat and strapped him in. She tucked his blankie under his chin, then turned to instruct Spud, "Take us straight to D/FW. Wait a minute—Love Field will be closer. Make that Love Field."

"Will do, Bosslady. We'll arrive about nine o'clock in the morning," he said, turning toward the cockpit.

A flight attendant came up to ask, "May I get you anything?"

Sitting in the seat beside Daniel, Adair groaned,

"Have you got a medical kit?" She picked up one lacerated foot.

The flight attendant brought a first-aid kit and helped Adair doctor the soles of her feet, then Adair asked, "Have you got any clothes on this crate?"

"No, I'm sorry; I didn't realize you would need any," the attendant said anxiously, with a quick involuntary look at the men's shorts.

"Okay; no problem," Adair sighed, reclining her seat to sleep near Daniel. "Wake me when we get there," she muttered, then she was out.

❧

Adair woke when the plane touched down. She knew she was on Texas soil now; she could feel it. She rose up to look out the window at the runway. Okay, she was home—but not home free. Those predators were here as well. How could she fight them without Fletcher?

She contemplated this question as she looked down on Daniel's little form curled up tight beside her. Then the realization of what she must do broke on her with such blinding clarity that she wondered why she had not thought of it before. The only question that remained was, could she do it?

The plane came to a stop and Spud appeared from the cockpit, looking tired and scruffy. "We're here, Mrs. Streiker."

She looked up. "Good. I need a taxi, and money for fare."

"Right away, Bosslady," he nodded and backed out. Meanwhile, the flight attendant came up with a tray of breakfast rolls, juice, and fruit.

Adair woke Daniel to have a bite. He looked around in confusion, twisting his blankie under his chin, but a smile from Adair put him at ease enough to accept a sugar-glazed roll. While they ate, he peered curiously out of the window.

"Cab's here, ma'am," Spud said, leaning in from the cockpit.

"Thank you," Adair said, stiffly getting up. Daniel sprang up like a wound toy to wrap his arms around her. Adair held him with one arm as she picked up his bag.

Spud extended two twenties to her. "That's all I got, Mrs. Streiker. Hope it's enough."

"If it won't be, the Whinnets will cover the rest," Adair said confidently. "Thank you, Spud," she added gratefully.

"Do you want me to keep the plane on standby for you?" Spud asked.

Adair looked at him, thinking. "No. I want you to go back to Hawaii and find Harle. When you do, he's to call me at the Whinnets'."

"Sure, Mrs. Streiker," Spud said with a slight note of unease.

Adair carried Daniel down the steps to the waiting cab. The driver eyed her with elevated brows, but she merely returned his gaze and said, "Ten seventy-three Papillon Court, here in Dallas."

"Whatever you say, lady," he replied, and took off.

Once in the cab Daniel's curiosity displaced his fear, and he peeked up from her shoulder to gaze out over the seas of shopping malls and housing developments they passed en route to the Whinnets' address. Adair asked quietly, "Have you ever seen Texas, Dan'l?" He laid his head back on her shoulder and she guessed he hadn't.

In about twenty minutes the taxi pulled up to the Whinnets' elegant home. Adair handed the driver the forty and asked, "Does that cover it?" He admitted it did and she said, "Good. You can go."

She gingerly carried the boy and the bag up the front cobbled walk, wincing at her sore feet. She rang the doorbell and waited. If they weren't here, she intended to sit on their front porch until they returned.

Alicia herself opened the door, and the surprise on her pixie face was immeasurable. "Why, Adair! You're—come in! We thought—who is this?" she asked, placing a tender hand on Daniel's bony back. He cemented himself to Adair.

"This is Fletcher's son Daniel," Adair said. Alicia stared at her with an almost uncomprehending gaze.

"Fletcher's son—! What?" said Charles, coming in from another room. "Adair, what's this all about? Where is Fletch?" he asked in alarm.

"Fletcher has disappeared, so I'm taking over his assets," Adair said. "I want you to show me what he's got and what you're doing with it."

C harles Whinnet stared at Adair with an expression of incredulousness almost identical to that of Alicia's. "Are you going to tell me I can't do that?" Adair demanded.

"No, of course not," he said, snapping out of his shock. "You just . . . caught me unprepared. What's this about Fletcher missing? What happened?"

"You didn't know?" Adair asked with vague suspicion.

"No, I swear," Charles said earnestly. "The last I talked with him was when he called from Honolulu. That would've been . . . Wednesday," he said, glancing at Alicia for verification.

Alicia nodded slowly, her eyes on the back of Daniel's head. He refused to raise his face from Adair's shoulder. "Fletcher's son," Alicia murmured. "Adair, tell us about him."

Adair shrugged, holding the precious little monkey.

"I don't know much. His mother wouldn't marry Fletcher, and spent all her time running away from him. She was killed in a car accident about a year ago. Fletcher was taking me to Hawaii to meet him." She recounted to them everything that had happened after he had called Charles—the funeral, the crash landing, her first meeting with Daniel, and the fire.

The Whinnets looked shaken. Charles, the tall, healthy tennis player, and lovely, petite Alicia stood gazing at the billionaire's bedraggled family. "My, he's full of surprises," Alicia observed with a weak laugh.

"This is serious," Charles admitted. "I was about to head downtown to negotiate the sale of the Streiker Building. I have power of attorney, but if word gets out that Fletcher is injured and missing, that could severely hamper our negotiations. Fletcher could lose millions—a billion—by the time everything is sold."

"No one that you're dealing with has to know," Adair said coolly. "If you'd normally have to call Fletcher to okay a deal, call me instead. Listen, I told Spud ["Who?" mused Alicia] to have Harle call me here with what he knows about Fletcher. Oh! And I want you to arrange to replace the Lokomaikai's house. But more important, I want investigators sent down there to find out how that fire started." As Adair talked, she dropped Daniel's bag to the floor. The little boy clamped his legs around her waist to prevent being put down.

"I'll get right on it and call you with what I find," Charles said with a quick nod. "Stay here for the time being."

"For a while," Adair agreed, as that was what she had in mind all along. Before he left, Charles reached out a hand to lightly stroke Daniel's black head. The boy recoiled, clutching Adair's neck so tightly that she almost choked. Charles quickly withdrew and went out to his car.

Alicia recovered from her shock to remember hospitality. "Are you hungry, Adair?" she wondered faintly.

Adair shook her head wearily, dropping into the closest overstuffed chair with Daniel. He lifted up slightly to rearrange his blankie under his chin; when he examined it and realized bunny was missing, a look of heartbroken alarm broke across his face. Adair reached down to his bag to retrieve bunny. Daniel accepted it with a sigh and nestled in her neck.

Alicia sat in a chair opposite them. "Why didn't Fletcher tell us about him?" she asked in a whisper.

Adair felt a wave of irritation. "Good question. I'd like to know why he didn't tell me, either. Part of the reason may be in the fact that Daniel's scared to death of him. I don't know when the last time was they saw each other, but just the mention of his name sends Daniel under the nearest piece of furniture."

"He loves you, though," Alicia said, her eyes resting on Daniel's backbone protruding through his T-shirt.

"We love each other. We're alone together," Adair said in some confusion of thought, but Daniel's stubby fingers reached up to touch her cheek. Adair shut her eyes and put her head back on the chair.

"You must be exhausted. Come up to the guest room and lie down. We'll put Daniel in the adjoining room," Alicia offered, standing.

"Thanks, but he has to stay with me." Adair stood with her burden. She glanced into the white drawing room. It was as new and clean and beautifully furnished as it was before Fletcher's old enemy showed up here with an Uzi. "I'm glad to see all the damage repaired. It was a mess," Adair remarked.

"Yes, but Fletcher took care of everything, just like

he said he would," Alicia said, turning toward the stairs.

Following her upstairs, Adair murmured, "Charles is arranging the sale of the building. If that goes through soon—Alicia, please call Reggie and have him bring Sugar over here. Ask her to pack another bag for me."

"Of course," Alicia said, opening the door to a pretty pink bedroom.

Adair pulled down the covers and sat Daniel on the bed. She took off his little sandals but he suddenly slipped down from the bed and trotted to the bathroom. He paused at the door, torn between his desire for privacy and his reluctance to be separated from Adair. So he eyed Alicia stonily.

She shook her head in wonder, musing, "He looks so much like him. Well—I'll leave you two to rest."

Adair nodded, "But wake me if Charles calls." Alicia assented, closing the door behind her on her way out.

Adair sank into the clean, soft sheets. In a few minutes she heard the toilet flush and felt bony knees crawling up on to the bed. "Did you wash your hands, Daniel?" she asked sleepily.

He wavered reluctantly, then padded back to the bathroom. She heard the faucet run for several seconds and the various sounds of childish labor. Then there were hurried lightweight footfalls and a small person all knees and elbows scampered into the bed and burrowed down at her side. Adair remembered removing his knees from her ribcage and encircling him with her arms before falling asleep.

⌒

"Adair, Charles is on the line," Alicia whispered in her ear.

Adair opened her eyes and took the cordless phone

Alicia held. "Hello," she said clearly. Anticipating this call even in her sleep, she was at once wide awake for it. Daniel, eyes shut fast, did not stir beside her.

"Okay, Boss, we've got a firm offer of 15 million for the building. It's not what I had hoped for, but with the vacancy rate downtown just over twenty percent, it's the best we can get. The restaurant chain can go for 130.5 million, and the plastics manufacturer for 36 million. We . . . already discussed the prospective buyers for these, remember?" Charles hinted.

"You mean, Fletcher has already okayed them," she guessed.

"That's right. Now, the highest bid we have received so far for the software company is 430 million—I don't like that at all; I think we should hold out on that one," said Charles. From his tone Adair deduced that his side of the conversation was being overheard.

"All right," she said.

"Done," he confirmed. "While I've got you on the line, let me recommend that we go ahead and invest these sums in fixed-asset accounts—interest rates are at six percent and appear likely to hold steady."

"Fine," she said, then remembered something from her accounting class: "How about marketable securities?"

He seemed caught off guard. "Uh—those have been fluctuating too much for my comfort level lately, but let me check into what's most stable right now."

"How much will you keep back for seed capital to invest in new start-ups?" she asked.

"At present, you have approximately 350 million in liquid assets. Are you comfortable with that?" Charles asked.

"I guess," she said. "What new ventures are at the

top of your list, and what do they require?"

"Yvonne has been screening those. Let me have her call you," Charles said. "Regarding your instructions this morning: I have sent two specialists on a plane to Maui. The damage estimates I have received indicate a total loss of the property in question at a value of 175 thousand, so I have wired a cash reimbursement to the property owners for that amount. I have left word for Harle, but I've received no further information on that situation." His voice faltered slightly at this point.

"Okay," she said softly, looking down at the sleeping child snuggled beside her.

"I will keep you informed as I know more," he said with a renewed edge in his voice.

"Thanks, Charles. Bye." Adair put the telephone down on the bedside table and replaced her arm around Daniel. He shifted, stuffing the blankie corner in his mouth.

A few minutes later the telephone warbled and Adair picked it up without thinking. "Hello?"

"Adair? It's Yvonne. Charles said you had a question about the applicants for venture assistance."

"Yes. Who's at the top of your list and how much do they need?" Adair asked.

"Well, our top contender is a communications company which has requested a 2.5 million dollar investment in exchange for equity in the company. They have a solid financial plan and cutting-edge technology," Yvonne related. "In descending order, our other applicants are a recycling plant requesting 500 thousand; an energy research company requesting 350 thousand; and a heart-disease research facility requesting 600 thousand," Yvonne related.

Mention of the last venture prompted Adair to ask, "What about all the charity requests Fletcher receives?"

Yvonne barely sighed. "I and *one* assistant are up to our feeble necks trying to sift though all the business proposals. The requests from charitable organizations have filled up the office next door. I can't begin to look at them."

"If the Streiker Building's being sold, where are you?" Adair asked.

"We're occupying another, smaller building which was purchased in mine and Charles's names," Yvonne replied.

"To house your business," Adair clarified.

"Yes, though we have not incorporated," Yvonne said.

"I see. Well, hire somebody to go through the charitable requests—somebody who knows Fletcher, and who has a good feel for what he would do and how he would do it—" Adair paused at a brainstorm. "Sugar. Hire Sugar to screen the requests from charities. She should be arriving here soon—"

Adair raised up as Alicia lightly knocked and opened the door. Adair waved her in. As Alicia entered, she set a suitcase down beside the bed.

"The question I had was," Adair continued, "is three hundred fifty million enough in liquid assets to carry on Fletcher's work?"

"Yes, I would think so," Yvonne said slowly. "Adair, it sounds like to me you need to be down here overseeing this operation."

Adair looked down at the responsibility sleeping beside her, the charge Fletcher declared with his last gasp as the most important thing in the world to him. "No . . . it's your baby. I've got to allow you room to do the job Fletcher gave you. Is . . . it okay with you to hire Sugar?"

"Of course," Yvonne replied.

"Great." Adair looked up to ask the waiting Alicia, "Is Sugar here?"

"Yes, downstairs," Alicia whispered. She kept glancing at Daniel curled up in Adair's side.

"Okay. Yvonne? Sugar's here. I'd like you to talk to her about what I suggested. And go ahead and fund those ventures, if they look good to you," Adair said.

"Will do gladly," Yvonne said. "Oh—before I forget: your mother called trying to reach Fletcher. She left her new number."

"Good. Give it to me," Adair said, scrounging for a pen and paper in the bedside table drawer. She found them and scribbled the number Yvonne relayed. "Thanks. Okay, I'm handing you over to Alicia," Adair said, then told Alicia around a yawn, "Tell Sugar that I hope she'll consider a job with Yvonne."

"I suppose she will," Alicia said. "She was shaken up to hear through the grapevine that the building's being sold."

Adair nodded sleepily, scooting back down under the covers. In his sleep Daniel rearranged his bunny under his chin. "When Yvonne and Sugar are done, bring me the phone. I need to call my mother . . . ," Adair murmured, closing her eyes, and Alicia quietly shut the door.

*

When Adair opened her eyes again, midafternoon sunshine streamed into the pink bedroom. She shifted and looked at Daniel sitting up beside her, chewing on his blankie. How long ago he had finished his nap she couldn't say, but he obviously wasn't about to start exploring this strange place without her. "You're a good little boy, Daniel," she yawned. "Fletcher will be so happy to see us getting along."

She said it without thinking, then quickly focused on him to see how he reacted. He merely chewed his blanket and looked out the window. Adair rolled onto her stomach and very gently disengaged the sodden blankie corner from his mouth. "Are you hungry?" she asked quietly.

He eyed her, his mouth clamped shut in fear or defiance. Adair strongly desired to see him laugh again—or at least smile, for pity's sake.

She sat up in bed, assuming a stern, rigid posture. With the appropriate hand motions, she began solemnly singing: "The itsy-bitsy spider crawled up the water spout; down came the rain and washed the spider out; up came the sun and dried up all the rain; and the itsy-bitsy spider crawled up the spout again."

The extent of Daniel's reaction was to blink once. Adair decided that a little boy would prefer more action. So again with the hand motions, she sang: "Little Rabbit Foo-Foo hopping through the forest, scooping up all the field mice and bashin' 'em on the head. Along comes the Good Fairy, and she says, 'Little Rabbit Foo-Foo, I don't want to see you scooping up all the field mice and bashin' 'em on the head. . . .'"

Daniel leaned back against the padded headboard and tried to sneak his blankie back in his mouth. Not an authority on children's songs, Adair had to rack her brain to come up with another. But then she remembered: "Do your ears hang low; do they wobble to and fro; can you tie them in a knot; can you tie them in a bow? Can you throw them over your shoulder like a Continental soldier; do your ears . . . hang . . . low?"

Daniel looked interested so Adair sang it again, faster, as she tied imaginary drooping ears under her chin and flung them over her shoulder. Daniel smiled and jiggled his leg. Adair sang it faster and Daniel suddenly dropped his blankie to mimic her hand motions.

She sang it again and again in attempting to get him to sing with her. He got proficient at the motions, but never opened his mouth. So Adair settled for what he was willing to give and after the sixth rendition of the song, grabbed him up for a big kiss. "I'm hungry! Let's go downstairs and see what Aunt Alicia has got for us!" Adair declared.

Daniel hopped down from the bed and went skipping out into the hall in front of her, saluting as a Continental soldier. Adair felt immensely gratified to see it. But then he ran smack into Jackie, the Whinnets' maid, as she emerged from another bedroom.

Jackie turned and looked down on him to say, "Why, I guess you're Mr. Streiker's little surprise, aren't you now?"

Daniel fled back to Adair in terror. She lifted him to her shoulder, smiling to Jackie. "Some surprise, huh?"

Jackie came up to pat him on the back affectionately. "I'm glad to meet you, kid. Knowin' 'bout you makes me like Mr. Streiker more. Makes me feel like I can call him Fletch. I think I will, next time I see him. 'Hi, Fletch. How's it going?'"

Adair laughed, "How so?"

"Well, you know, he always seemed a little too perfect. He always intimidated the heck out of me. But—an illegitimate child?" Jackie raised her brows scandalously. "So maybe he's human after all. Then again, somebody as rich as him could just pay off a problem and get it out of his life. But he didn't. He brought him to you and said, 'This kid is mine. Please love him.' You have to respect that. Somehow, it makes me respect him more than if he'd never made a mistake in his life."

Adair rocked Daniel lightly on her shoulder as she thought this over. "When Charles first told me about him, he said Fletcher lived by a moral code that left most people in the dust. Now I'm wondering if . . . this is the reason why," she said, squeezing him gently, ". . . if having Daniel made him that way."

"Who's to say?" said Jackie, shrugging. "But *I* just made a hot apple pie. And we have vanilla ice cream to go on top. No child in the world has ever refused Jackie's hot apple pie á la mode."

"Oh, stop," Adair moaned. "We're on our way right now."

They hustled downstairs where Jackie served up great slabs of pie and ice cream. As Alicia entered the kitchen Daniel received the first piece, and three soft-hearted women had the supreme satisfaction of watching a hungry child attack apple pie. Unable to move the fork adroitly but knowing that he was supposed to use it, Daniel guided chunks onto his fork with his fingers before shoveling them in his mouth. But he could not get to all the apple pieces with the ice cream in the way, and he could not lift the whole scoop with his fork. So finally he put the fork down to stand on his knees in the chair and plant his mouth on the blob of melting ice cream. Adair turned away to hide her snickers.

Jackie took a spoon from the drawer and used it to break up his ice cream into manageable chunks. Daniel readily accepted help from the lady who made apple pie, who swaggered a bit at being put on his okay list.

When the ice cream was disposed of, Alicia gently reintroduced Daniel to the fork. He gazed at her, the lower half of his face and part of his nose coated with ice cream. But he took the fork to finish off the pie.

Alicia was beaming as she turned from him to Adair.

"I'm sorry I didn't wake you after Sugar left, but—you looked so tired."

"Is she going to work for Yvonne?" Adair asked.

"Yes, she and Reggie both. He took her to Yvonne's new office, where he was hired as a courier," Alicia said.

"Good. Great!" Adair said, pulling up a chair beside Daniel. She was glad Sugar would not be doing housework for a living anymore, with her arthritis. Adair watched Daniel as she thought about the rapid changes in her friends' situations. It seemed that everybody had a new job. Adair understood why Daniel was so important to Fletcher, and she accepted the responsibility of taking care of him, but she couldn't help feeling . . . well, out of the loop. Insignificant. Recalling Charles's incredulity when she said she was taking over Fletcher's assets, she wondered if he would have reacted the same if she had shown up in a suit, without a child in tow.

"Doesn't matter," she sighed. Daniel finished his pie and then looked around shyly. He was surrounded by adults and beautiful adult things—nothing he could put his little hands on. When Alicia approached him with a damp paper towel for his face, he hopped from his chair into the protection of Adair's lap.

Alicia looked hurt, but gave the towel to Adair to wash his face. "Why is he so frightened?" Alicia wondered.

"I . . . think it has to do with his mother's poor relationship with Fletcher," Adair said, wiping down the upturned face and fingers. "But Harle didn't know much and Daniel isn't saying."

Daniel's small hands fidgeted for blankie and bunny, but as they were upstairs, he twisted his fingers in the excess folds of Adair's shirt. "I wish I had something for you to play with," she said regretfully.

"How about some homemade play dough?" Jackie asked.

Adair looked up. "Do you have some?"

"I have a recipe," Jackie said, flipping open a big book. "Doesn't take much—flour, salt, food coloring. Takes about fifteen minutes to whip up."

"Jackie, you have to cook all the time. Let me make it," Adair said, lifting Daniel from her lap to another chair. She came over to the counter where Jackie laid out the recipe.

"Okay, honey." Jackie pulled out a Dutch oven from a low drawer and food coloring from a high shelf. "Pick a color."

Adair took the choices over to Daniel, who was looking on with great interest from the table. "What color do you want the play dough, Daniel?" she asked. He looked at her in puzzlement, but picked up the blue bottle. "Blue it is," she declared.

As Adair scooped out flour to the large pan, Daniel dragged his chair over to stand on it and watch. She measured out salt and let him pour it into the pan. Then she had him add the food coloring to the water. He watched the deep blue eddies swirl in the clear water and looked up with shining eyes. Adair hugged him. *Now, what job could have more perks than this?* she thought.

He observed closely as she stirred the dough mixture around the hot pan until it got thicker and thicker. Then she turned it out to knead it gingerly on the counter. Unable to resist, he stuck a finger in the pretty blue dough and promptly pulled it back in surprise at the warmth. "Still hot. Careful," she murmured. "See?" She showed him her red palms.

In a few minutes it was cool and smooth. Jackie found some utensils, and shortly Daniel was engrossed

139

in play dough. He kneaded and pounded and made snakes to squish and tall towers to knock over. He made millions of little balls. Adair watched him in satisfaction, sitting down to finally eat her piece of pie. Seeing him play reminded her of Brian. That made her remember—"Oh, I need to call my mom. Left the number upstairs." She got up to fetch it, but as soon as she started out of the doorway Daniel leaped from his seat and fastened himself to her leg.

"Daniel, it's okay; I'll be right back," Adair assured him, but he wouldn't let go.

"Never mind; I'll go get it," Jackie said. "You sit down and eat your pie before it gets any cooler." Adair could not see any reason to argue with her. Adair sat, and Daniel laboriously dragged his heavy swivel chair right up next to hers to resume his play.

As Adair ate, she remembered eating here before, waiting to hear from Fletcher. Suddenly she looked around with a start, cocking her head. "What is it?" Alicia asked.

"Where is Panny? The dog Fletcher brought over here?" Adair wondered.

"He asked us to put an ad in the lost-and-found section of the paper. The owners saw it and came for him a few days ago. They were so relieved, and—frankly, so was I," Alicia admitted.

"He thinks of everything," Adair mused. "He follows through on little things nobody else would bother about." Suddenly she felt not quite so abandoned.

Jackie entered with the telephone and scrawled number, which she handed over. "Thanks," Adair said, adding as she dialed, "I'm not really excited about this. Last time I talked to my mom she was in such a snit because Fletcher had bought them everything they asked for and they didn't know what to do with it all."

She put the telephone to her ear and listened as it was answered, "Hello?"

"Hi, um, Brian? This is Adair."

"Oh, hi, Adair! How ya doin'?" he said happily.

"Fine, just fine. I had a message that Mom called, and I was just . . . returning her call," Adair said.

"Mom and Dad aren't here. They took the boat down to the marina, and I had to stay here with a baby-sitter," he said, pouting.

"Oh, did they find a place to store the boat?" Adair asked.

"Kinda. See, they're talkin' to somebody 'bout donating the boat to the city for them to use it for the old folks' get-togethers and some kind of charity deals, and we get to use it whenever we want to. Mom was real happy—the paper came out to do an article about it and Dad had to get dressed up to go talk to these guys, or something, and he didn't like that, but gettin' rid of that boat from out in front of the house made every-body real happy," he related.

"Brian, what a wonderful thing to do! I'm so glad that worked out. What about the other problems?" Adair asked.

"Gee, things have settled down a lot. Dad was just crazy about the taxes he'd have to pay on all the stuff, but he took care of a lot of that when he gave a chunk of money to this hospital, and then he did a prepay, or something, so that's not such a big deal as we thought," Brian said. "And they decided they didn't want another house, but Mom got new carpet and she's happy as can be."

"Brian, that's great. Well. I'm so surprised they got everything worked out like that. I wouldn't have thought they could do it," Adair admitted.

"I don't think they woulda all by themselves," Brian hedged.

"What do you mean?" Adair asked.

He replied, "I mean without Fletch's help. He called and talked to them a long time about it this morning. That's how they knew what to do."

# 10

Adair's mouth hung open for fifteen seconds. "Brian—are you sure it was Fletcher? Did you talk with him?"

"Nuh-uh, I was at school. Mom said that he called and that they talked to him for at least an hour," Brian said.

"How did he get your number? Did you write him and give him your new number?" Adair demanded.

"No, I just got his letter the other day. I guess Mom gave it to him; I don't know," Brian said.

Adair was flummoxed. "Well . . . I'm glad . . . everything worked out so well. Brian, let me give you my number here, and ask Mom to call me. Also, if you hear from Fletcher again, please call me."

"Gee, Adair, isn't he with you?" Brian asked.

"Um, not at the moment." She clearly dictated the Whinnets' number to him and asked, "Do you have that down?"

"Yeah. No problem," he said.

"Okay. Thanks, Brian. Bye." Adair slowly hung up. "He said Fletcher called and talked to my parents this morning," she told Alicia in a monotone.

"I don't understand," Alicia said faintly.

"I don't either," Adair whispered, bowing her head. In spite of her efforts to be strong and self-controlled, this latest spin was too much. The tears began slipping down her face.

In distress, Daniel abandoned the play dough to climb into her lap. When Adair saw the anxiety in his face she instantly commanded her eyes to dry up. "I'm sure there is an explanation," she said.

"It may not have been Fletcher at all," Alicia said hastily. "It could have been someone posing as him."

Adair thought about that. "Perhaps. Only . . . my parents have met him and talked to him. They know what he sounds like. And I'm afraid that what they did sounds just like something he would tell them to do—if the boat's a problem, give it to someone who can turn it into an asset."

She held Daniel's troubled face. "Your daddy is a good man, and he loves us. I know that. If he's contacted somebody else but not us, I *know* there must be a reason for it—" She broke off as something occurred to her. "He said . . . when we were in Hawaii, he said there were predators, and he was a killdeer. He said he intended to lure the predators away from his business—"

Adair caught her breath. "I thought he was talking about his *business*—the company! But that doesn't mean anything to him—he's selling it all off! He was talking about the business that he wanted me to handle! He was talking about Daniel! He's trying to protect Daniel!" she exclaimed.

Adair gripped the boy. "Don't you see?" she whispered. "That has to be it! Someone shot at our helicopter on our way to see you. Fletcher wanted to keep them away from you, so he left, but not before he made sure I would find you. He won't contact us because it's not safe yet. But—it's okay for him to call my parents in Longview. That way we'll know he's all right. He's telling us not to worry, Daniel!"

Daniel put his head down and covered his ears. "I know," she sighed, kissing the babyish hands. "Some things are too hard for us to hear."

Alicia sat digesting this, then said, "Charles needs to know about this. He needs to know not to tell anyone you're here."

"I agree," Adair said, and Alicia picked up the telephone to call her husband.

Adair looked down at the boxer shorts with the troublesome gap. "I've got to change. I hope Sugar brought me a decent pair of jeans."

Alicia moved the telephone away from her mouth. "You can wear anything of mine you like."

"Uh—thanks," Adair said, getting up with Daniel. She was afraid nothing of Alicia's would fit her. "Let me see what Sugar brought." She set Daniel down and he gathered up his play dough. As she started up the stairs he was right behind her, carrying it with him.

Adair paused, hiding a smile. "Um, Aunt Alicia, Daniel would like to keep his play dough. Do you have something he could put it in?"

On hold, Alicia put down the phone and brought him a plastic bag which he gravely accepted, and Adair helped him stash his play dough in it. Upstairs, as she knelt to open her suitcase (her old one, as the two new tapestry bags were sitting in Fletcher's house in Honolulu), Daniel stored his new toy in his nylon bag.

Presciently, Sugar had packed Adair's favorite jeans and a slouchy sweater. Adair took them to the bathroom to change, talking to Daniel in a chatty, reassuring manner: "Well, big guy, your shorts and T-shirts were fine for the islands, but if we stay here for any length of time I'm going to have to get you some warmer clothes! How about a Cowboys sweatshirt? Every boy in Dallas needs a Cowboys sweatshirt or two."

Dressed, she came out and sat on the bed to put on socks and her lace-up ankle boots. She noticed Daniel foraging with increasing anxiety in the bedcovers. "What . . . ? Oh, you're missing bunny and blankie, aren't you? Well, I know we left them right here. Let's go ask Jackie if she's seen them."

Adair stretched out her arms and Daniel readily climbed up in them. As she carried Daniel down the stairs, they met Jackie coming up. "Jackie, have you seen Mr. Blankie and Mr. Bunny?"

"Yes, I have. Messrs. Blankie and Bunny were screaming for a bath, so I put 'em in the washer. They're drying now with a nice, soft load of sheets and towels," Jackie said.

"Thank you," Adair breathed. Daniel looked grieved. "Jackie, could you do something else for us? Dan'l here needs some Dallas wear. Could you . . . ?"

Jackie scrutinized the scrawny figure. "Go shopping? You dialed the right number. C'mon, Tiger, want to go with Aunt Jackie?" She held out her arms, but Daniel buried his face on Adair's neck.

"I don't guess he's ready for that yet. Why don't you just take a change of his clothes to judge the size? And Jackie"—Adair took her arm—"he needs *every-thing*."

"Gotcha," Jackie said, lifting her stately frame on up the stairs. "You might tell the missus we'd better order in dinner tonight."

Adair glanced back at her with a puckered smile—Jackie was not one to strain herself—and headed on downstairs.

Alicia came from the kitchen. "I just got off the phone with Charles. He thinks your idea is plausible, as he's heard nothing from anyone in Hawaii since Fletcher called Wednesday."

"What is today?" Adair blinked.

"Friday. Listen—," Alicia began, but the telephone rang. Jackie was heading down the stairs so Alicia turned back to the kitchen to answer it. With a strange face, she brought out the telephone a moment later. "It's for you," she said, handing it to Adair.

"Hello?" she answered, her gut tightening.

"Bosslady. It's Spud." His voice was low and they had a poor connection.

"Spud? What is it? What have you found out?" Adair asked rapidly.

"I found Harle. He's in the hospital—shot in the back and the neck. There's some big *pilikia* here, and—"

"What? I can't understand you," Adair said, pressing the receiver closer to her ear.

"Trouble, Bosslady. Things don't look too good here. You better stay off the islands for a while," he said.

"How is Harle? Will he be all right?" she asked anxiously.

"Uh, yeah, I guess. But we got monster waves rolling in and you need to stay on the shore. Laydahs, Bosslady." The line went dead.

Adair quietly put the phone down. Her tension was translated directly to Daniel, who squeezed her neck relentlessly. Adair forced herself to relax and rubbed his back. "It's okay, Daniel. We did the right thing coming here."

She glanced up at Alicia's worried face and said calmly, "That was Fletcher's mechanic. Harle has been shot. He's in the hospital. I guess he couldn't tell Spud much of anything, but Spud warned me to stay away from the islands."

"You'll stay right here. This is the safest place for you," Alicia decreed.

Adair nodded slightly, watching Daniel twine his fingers in her sweater. "Aunt Alicia, where is your washer and dryer? We're expecting our friends to come out shortly."

Smiling, Alicia took them back to a spacious laundry room off the kitchen. Alicia leaned over the dryer to look at the timer. "This load will be dry in about five minutes," she announced. With his back against the wall opposite the dryer, Daniel slid down to a sitting position and intently watched the machine hum.

Adair sat beside him. "We'll wait here. Thank you, Aunt Alicia." She eyed Daniel as they waited. This would be a good time to talk to him, but she did not know what to say. So for now she let the purring of the dryer fill the silence.

The timer buzzed. Daniel got right up and opened the dryer to dig through the warm sheets. He found his blankie and pressed it against his face. It was up to Adair to locate bunny, tied up in a pillowcase. When she untied it and freed a soft, fuzzy, sweet-smelling bunny, Daniel's face glowed.

A cold front swept into town late that afternoon, which caused the house's heating system to come on. Vaguely restless, Daniel wandered around the ground floor of the house. He looked through the back door and spotted the landscaping pebbles around the back porch. These intrigued him, so he ventured to open the door to go out. But the cold air which rushed in from the deceptively sunny outdoors caused him to slam the door and wrap his blankie around his thin shoulders.

So Adair was heartily grateful to see Jackie breeze in from her shopping trip laden with bags. Even Daniel edged forward curiously as Jackie brought out jeans, sweatshirts, and crew socks. But the biggest hit was unquestionably the high-topped sneakers with neon orange laces. Daniel promptly dropped bunny and blankie to seize the shoes and put them on his bare feet. They were slightly too big and made his legs look even more like brown sticks, but he was now 2 Cool. He walked around with his head down watching his shoes for the next ten minutes.

While Jackie gave all her receipts to Alicia, Adair coaxed Daniel out of his shoes long enough to put jeans and socks on him. Topped off with a Batman sweatshirt and the glorious shoes, he looked like any spoiled suburban kid. "Wow, Dan'l, look at you!" Adair marveled, turning him around to a mirror on the closet door.

Daniel gazed at his reflection, fingering the Batman logo on the front of his shirt. Then he grinned at Adair in the mirror as she stood proudly behind him. He returned his gaze to his new appearance, his grin settling into a contemplative smile of satisfaction. Even though he had not said a word, Adair considered it abundant thanks.

Charles arrived home shortly thereafter, and they called in to a favorite Chinese restaurant that delivered. But when Charles turned toward Daniel, the child scampered to the safety of Adair's lap.

"Show Uncle Chuck your shoes, Dan'l," she urged in a whisper. "He'll want to see your shoes."

Dubiously, Daniel peeked out from Adair's arms. Charles looked over in exaggerated surprise. "Who's that big kid?" he demanded. "Where's the little boy I left this morning?" So Daniel slipped from Adair's lap to saunter over and point at his shoes. Seeing them, Charles squinted and shaded his eyes. "Man, somebody get my sunglasses!" Daniel actually cackled as he ran back to Adair.

When their dinner arrived, Daniel took his place at the table like a regular person and eagerly pointed to the noodles. Adair noted that he even knew how to use chopsticks—better than a fork, actually.

Over dinner, Charles quietly informed them, "So far so good. Word about the sell-off has spread so that we're getting inundated with offers, and prices are holding. Alicia told me about the call from Hawaii, Adair," he mentioned, nodding toward his wife. "Let's just pray that nothing from there hits the papers over here."

Adair nodded tensely. "I feel like you know Fletcher better than I do—"

"Not necessarily," Charles interrupted, glancing at Daniel.

"I mean," Adair continued, trying not to become distracted, "do you really think it's possible that Fletcher's okay, and just staying away to protect us?"

Charles's brows drew together. "Yeah, sure, it's possible, but I can't help feeling there's more to it than that."

Adair slumped. "You can't mean that he's staying away to give me more training in making decisions without him."

"Oh no. This is not training. This is the real thing,

150

and the stakes are sky-high," Charles said seriously. Adair bit her lip and looked at Daniel devouring the noodles.

After dinner, Charles and Alicia had a social function scheduled. Alicia was reluctant to leave Adair, and Charles did not want to go period, but Adair begged—insisted—that they keep their engagement.

Eventually they had to admit the wisdom of keeping up appearances, and shortly after Jackie had left for the evening, they changed into formal wear and pulled out in their Mercedes. Adair and Daniel were left alone in the big house.

Suddenly it was very quiet. Daniel sat on the couch with his blankie and bunny, swinging his legs. He kept looking out the door toward the landscaped backyard with its interesting pebbles. By now it was dark out, and Adair never considered the possibility that he would want to venture out there again.

She looked around for something to interest a four-year-old. The Whinnets had a large-screen television set and a number of movies. Adair sat in front of the video cabinet to look through them. "Let's see . . . *Casablanca*, *Gone with the Wind*, *My Fair Lady*—you'll enjoy those in about twenty years. . . . Oh, look, Daniel, they have *The Little Mermaid*! Would you like to see—" She turned around to the couch and Daniel was gone.

"Daniel?" Uneasily, she got up to look for him. "Daniel! If you're not going to answer me at least come when I call. Daniel!" She looked in the kitchen and front rooms, but he was not there. She trotted up the stairs to look in the pink bedroom and the bathroom, but he was not there.

"Daniel!" Vexed and slightly frightened, she ran back down the stairs. Then she saw the back door ajar. Starting toward it, she suddenly remembered King

Herod, the Whinnets' Doberman pinscher which ruled the back yard. He was so ill-tempered that Jackie was the only one who could control him.

As Adair reached the back door she saw Daniel bending over the pebbles around the porch and the black shadow of the Doberman silently lunging toward him. Adair opened her mouth to cry out but her throat closed up in a spasm. King Herod reached Daniel and Adair shot out of the house.

An instant later the dog had knocked Daniel down and stood over him. The boy lay still, gazing up at the huge dog breathing in his face through bared teeth. Adair halted near them, calculating how to get Daniel safely away from the dog.

Slowly, Daniel reached up and patted the animal's massive head. King Herod sniffed his face. At once his stubby tail began wriggling and he lolled out a giant tongue to wash down Daniel's face and ears.

Letting out a shaky breath, Adair inched forward to wedge her way between them. She cautiously pushed King Herod away with one hand while she took Daniel's arm with the other. "Good dog. Nice King Herod. Nice puppy," she rambled in a steady voice. She lifted Daniel with one arm, keeping the dog at bay, and carried him into the house.

Once inside the house with the back door bolted, Adair almost collapsed. "Daniel, don't ever do that to me again!" she cried, and he stared at her in dismay. To make amends, he dug in his pocket and brought out a handful of pebbles as a peace offering.

"You monkey!" she exclaimed in a half laugh, half sob. She seized him and covered him with violent kisses while he manfully tried to hold on to the pebbles. But he lost them in the struggle and was moved to protest deep in Adair's embrace.

"What?" she gasped, letting go to look at him. "Daniel, did you say something? Talk to me, baby, please!" He gazed at her through the deep brown eyes of his father and parted his lips. But then the curtain came down again, and he knelt to pick up his scattered prizes.

Wordlessly, Adair helped him find every little pebble. Her heart ached at how close he had come—a hairbreadth—from talking. *Be patient*, she told herself. *Just be patient and love him.*

When all the pebbles had been recovered, Adair put on *The Little Mermaid* and sat Daniel in her lap to watch it. Daniel was entranced, of course, and Adair was mesmerized as well. There was something in poor Ariel's desire to be more than she was, to escape the confinement of the sea and walk on human legs, that struck a deep chord of sympathy in Adair's own heart.

There was a discordant note intruding into the music; Adair turned her head to listen. It was the front doorbell. Frowning, Adair scooted Daniel off her lap onto the couch. "I've got to see who's at the door. I'll be right back. And Dan'l—*don't go anywhere*." She shook her finger at him and he looked up innocently.

Adair quietly went to the front door and leaned on it to look through the peephole. As the house was ringed with bright security lights, she could see the man outside quite clearly without turning on the porch light. He wiped his face nervously and rang the doorbell again.

Adair studied him suspiciously. He wore a casual, well-made sports coat. In his late forties, he had been a good-looking man at one time, but the bloodshot eyes and red, pulpy nose marked him as a heavy drinker.

Absolutely disinclined to open the door, Adair waited for him to go away. He rapped the door knocker now, jingling keys or coins anxiously in his pocket as he waited. He continued to stand there and Adair continued to watch him until he made an idiosyncratic gesture of throwing his arm out to raise his sleeve so he could look at his watch.

Adair unlocked the door and threw it open. "Daddy?" she asked, peering at him. She was astounded that his face would have changed so much in ten years as to be unrecognizable to her.

"Adair!" He broke into one of those rare, happy smiles from the old days.

⟋

"**D**addy!" She flung her arms around his neck and he squeezed her tightly. "Daddy, what are you doing here? How did you know I was here? Come in!" She stepped back from the door.

Her father came in timidly, glancing around the luxurious marble foyer. "Well, I called your mom in Longview today to see if she'd heard from you lately, and she told me you were staying with friends here. [Adair paused to wonder why her mother had not returned her call, then decided that Dana wouldn't bother if Fletcher weren't here.] I've been trying to get hold of you ever since I read about your wedding. Congratulations, sweetheart."

"Thanks, Daddy." She leaned forward to receive his kiss on the cheek and smelled the alcohol on his breath. Discouraged but polite, she pointed back into the house. "Come on back. Would you like something to eat?"

"Sure, I guess so, if it's not too much trouble," he said humbly. As he followed her back to the kitchen he mentioned, "I didn't think anyone was ever going to answer the door. Isn't anyone else here?"

"Well, my husband is out of town on business, and

the Whinnets had to go to a party tonight," Adair said. On hearing this, her father relaxed considerably. Adair leaned into the television room to check on Daniel, who looked up from the couch.

Her father stepped in and saw Daniel. "Well, who's this?" he asked. Adair got the immediate, uncomfortable impression that he was feigning.

She walked over to the couch and put her hand on Daniel's smooth black head. He gazed up at her in utter trust and she said, "This is my son."

"Oh. I see," said her father with craggy brows raised. "Hello there, young man. Carl Weiss." He came forward, extending his hand. Daniel leaned back against Adair and crammed his blankie in his face.

She hugged him reassuringly as she settled him back on the couch. "He's kind of shy."

Rounding the couch to go to the kitchen, Adair gestured her father to follow. "Now, let's see what we have," she said, opening the refrigerator.

"Here, Adair, you sit down and don't wait on me. I'll just help myself," he urged. So Adair sat at the table while Carl rummaged through the refrigerator. He brought out a can of caviar and a bottle of good white wine, then sat with these and a box of crackers from the counter.

Adair bit her lip and asked, "What brings you around, Dad?"

He loaded caviar on a cracker and glanced up. "Well, honey, let me shoot straight with you. Your old man's business bit the big one a few years back. Yeah, lemme tell you, the competition out there is just cutthroat. Guys'll slit your throat for a chance to make a buck. It's tough. But now, I've got a line on a business brokerage deal. It's a sure thing. Why, the projected earnings will knock your socks off." He chomped down on a cracker.

"Let me see them," Adair said quietly.

"Eh?" He looked up through his red eyes.

"Let me see the projections. Is this a franchise? Let me see a portfolio and a business plan," she said.

Carl wiped his hands and laughed drily. "Well, uh, honey, this is a little bit beyond you. Frankly, I was hoping to talk to your old man about this."

"He's not here right now, so you'll have to talk to me," Adair said softly. "What have you got on paper to show me?"

A brief flash of anger flicked through his eyes. He relaxed and laughed. "Now, Adair, are you going to make *me* give you a song and a dance? This is your father talking, sweetheart. Can't you just take my word for it that this is a sure thing?"

Adair looked down, then asked, "How much do you want?"

"Oh, I'd say ten million will get me started in a bare-bones operation," he said with a perfectly straight face.

Adair did not blink. "That's a lot of money."

"It takes money to make money," he observed, dipping his cracker directly into the can.

"And would this be a grant or a loan?" she asked.

He looked at her with wounded pride. "Of course I'd pay him back. I'd have enough after my third sale to pay him back with interest, at the going market rate."

Adair studied his lined, dissipated face. "All right, then. We'll have Charles draw up the papers in the morning."

"What papers?" he asked in alarm.

"The terms of the loan, of course," Adair said.

Now he got angry. "You expect me to sign papers to pay him back? I'm your father!"

"If you intend to pay it back, why should you object

to putting it in writing?" Adair asked calmly.

He got up and began to pace. "You—greedy little disrespectful sleaze! Here's your father, down on his luck, without a dollar to his name, and you go demanding to make sure I pay back whatever you lend me when your old man throws away millions on jets and houses in Hawaii and whatever else he wants! What have you become? What happened to my little girl who used to wait at the door for me to come home after work?"

Adair was pierced through the heart. Lowering her head, she said tearfully, "I'm sorry, Daddy. I'll get you whatever you need to get back on your feet."

He nodded gruffly and sat back at the table. "That's better. Don't cry, sweetheart. Your old dad got a little upset and said some nasty things. We'll work it out, sweetie." He patted her with a trembling hand.

Adair nodded and wiped her eyes. "So . . . ," he said, and opened his hands. "Can you get me the cash?"

She looked up in astonishment. "Tonight? Daddy, I can't get you anything till the banks open in the morning."

He seemed aggrieved. "Well . . . I thought you'd be able to call them up any time to get what you want. With that much money, you oughta be able to!"

She shrugged helplessly. "Fletcher himself couldn't get in the banks' timed vaults until the morning. I . . . guess I could get my hands on some cash tonight, if Fletcher has left any with Charles. But we still have to wait until the Whinnets get home to open their safe."

"Well. . . ." Carl wiped his face and looked away. Then he looked toward the kitchen doorway and smiled in an unpleasant imitation of kindliness. Adair turned and saw Daniel standing in the doorway, clutching his bunny and blankie. He was watching Carl with distinct mistrust.

Adair got up from her chair and lifted Daniel to her neck, rocking him tenderly. Carl eyed them and asked, "So whose boy is he?"

Adair blinked, then softly replied, "Mine. He's mine." She took him to the couch to continue watching the movie.

A moment later Carl entered the room and began pacing behind the couch. Daniel coiled up on Adair's lap. Carl paced and breathed behind them, impatiently checking his watch. "Say, what time do you expect these people back?"

Adair shook her head slightly. "Probably not for hours yet." She looked up at the fine old clock ticking on the mantel and tensed at the thought of her father waiting here for Charles and Alicia. She did not want him here a moment longer.

Turning, she suggested, "Listen, since they won't be here till late, why don't you go get some sleep and come back in the morning?"

"Oh, no, you're not gettin' rid of me that easy," he snarled. "We're waitin' right here till they come home." He placed his hand on her shoulder, digging his fingers into her collarbone until she winced.

# ⟨ 11 ⟩

**A**dair sat stiffly on the couch, shielding Daniel while Carl paced the room. He looked over the knick-knacks lining the shelves, which included some very fine antique porcelain. Then he glanced back at Adair with a downright malicious smile.

Watching him, she grew increasingly uneasy. She had not seen him for years and knew very little about his life now. What she had learned in the past half hour was not encouraging.

Besides his greed and obvious intemperance, there was something else that disturbed her deeply. There was something that didn't add up, but she couldn't quite figure it out. . . .

Until she thought about Daniel. Cuddling him, she had to smile and wonder at what point she decided he was hers. Somehow, it didn't bother her for her father to think she had a child out of wedlock. It was more important to her to protect Daniel. But why should she feel she had to protect him from her father? Daniel was obviously a child of the islands, with little connection to anyone outside of Hawaii.

*How did he know Fletcher has a house in Hawaii?* The question hit Adair with a dull, resounding thud. As she watched Carl lean on the French doors to look out into the backyard, the answer came with such swift certainty that it almost knocked her breathless. *He knows because he's been there.* Without a doubt, Adair now knew that it was Carl's voice over the intercom at Fletcher's home, arguing with Nona about seeing him.

Adair calmly stroked Daniel's glossy black hair. He was no longer watching the movie; instead, his eyes warily followed Carl's every move. *He knows an enemy when he sees one*, she thought with a chill.

Now, assuming that Carl was indeed at Fletcher's house in Honolulu, then how did he get there? He said he did not have a dollar to his name, and Adair believed him. Undoubtedly, he had drunk it all. So someone else must have paid for his airfare and someone else must have pointed out the house, or at least the area, in which Fletcher resided. Someone else had sent this predator to the nest.

At this point Adair was torn between finding out who had hired him and getting him out of the house. That indecision was short-lived, however; Carl was growing increasingly agitated and impatient. "Look," he said, wheeling, "maybe I don't need the ten million right away. Five hundred thousand will do tonight."

"I can't get to a dime of it until the Whinnets get back," Adair maintained. Actually, she knew she could call Yvonne to get it, but there was no need to tell him that. Adair guessed that extorting a chunk of money out of her was not in the original plan; this was a side-line which he wished to pursue before fulfilling his contractual obligations. Studying his buttoned sports coat, she came to the conclusion that he was carrying a gun.

In a sudden fit he knocked a vase of mums from its stand, sending it crashing in a wet array of shards and flowers across the marble floor. Daniel hunched down in Adair's lap, trembling. His fear armed Adair to the teeth and she looked up with eyes of steel at her father.

"Where are they?" Carl demanded. "I want you to call them and tell them they need to come home right now!"

"Let me see if I can find the number," she said calmly, dislodging Daniel from her lap. As he clung stubbornly to her neck, she whispered in his ear, "Open the back door and call the dog in." His arms loosened slightly and she nodded purposefully at him, glancing at the door.

Adair went over to a desk to begin rummaging for an address book, then paused. "Did I hear their car? Let me check." With Carl close on her heels, she went to the front door, unlocked it and looked out. "No, I guess it wasn't them," she said in disappointment. She was careful not to close the door all the way when she came back inside.

She returned to the television room to see Daniel standing at the back door, holding it open. King Herod was bounding toward the open door. With a dancer's quickness Adair leaped to Daniel and snatched him out of the way. A split second later the Doberman crossed the threshold. With no inkling as to whether the dog would obey her, Adair thrust a finger toward Carl entering the room and shouted, "Sic him! Get him, King Herod!"

The dog streaked past her with graceful, mighty strides. Carl was already running for his life toward the front door. He managed to make it out to the sidewalk before King Herod blindsided him, knocking him down on his face.

Adair stood at the door and whistled. King Herod paused and looked back. "That's a good boy! Here, boy! Here, King!" she called. Daniel came up behind her to clutch her leg and the Doberman left his prey on the sidewalk to trot up to the house, tail wriggling.

Adair dragged him inside and locked the door. "Good boy! Good boy!" she exclaimed, rubbing him vigorously. He sniffed her arm but licked Daniel, who patted the monstrous head with stubby baby fingers. Remembering the back door, Adair ran back and locked it as well. She turned to Daniel behind her with King Herod in tow. "Good going, Dan'l! Let's get ol' King Herod a treat."

So she went to the freezer and found a sirloin steak. She thawed it in the microwave until it was just warm and bloody, then fed it to King Herod on the kitchen floor. Holding each other tightly, Adair and Daniel sat back down to watch the rest of the movie.

When the Whinnets returned from their soirée in the wee hours of Saturday morning, they were perplexed to find Daniel and Adair asleep on the television room sofa and King Herod curled up on the floor beside them. While Charles ushered the recalcitrant, whining Doberman out to the backyard, Alicia found a blanket to cover her guests without waking them.

⁓

The following morning there was a long conference about what had happened the previous night. Jackie accidentally let the flapjacks burn as she hovered over Adair telling how her father had blustered his way in with guilt and threats. Charles and Alicia listened quietly until she was finished, then they watched Daniel devour pancakes as they contemplated the episode.

"I'm sorry about the vase," Adair added. "Please be sure to deduct its value from Fletcher's accounts."

Charles shook his head vaguely. "It's not valuable— just a reproduction. Did he really expect that you would be able to hand over half a million in cash last night?"

"I guess so," Adair said, raising her shoulders. "When I convinced him I couldn't get to anything in the bank until the morning, he seemed willing to settle for whatever you had in your safe. By that time I knew I had to get him out of the house. Now I'm wondering if he's going to show up this morning to take you and me to the bank!"

Charles looked at her. "Why would you need me?"

"To access Fletcher's accounts, of course, since you have power of attorney," Adair replied. She accepted a plate of fresh, hot pancakes from Jackie with an appreciative smile.

Charles and Alicia exchanged glances, and he said, "Adair, didn't you realize you have signature authority on all of Fletcher's accounts?" She stared at him and he added for emphasis, "You've had it since the day you were married. Didn't Harb Bayles tell you this? You don't need me or anybody else to get to Fletcher's money."

Adair paused with the pitcher of maple syrup poised over her plate. Daniel looked at her, looked at the pitcher, then assisted her in tipping it so that it poured a generous amount of syrup over her pancakes. "But—," she floundered, "you know, when I tried to withdraw five thousand dollars through the money machine for a mink coat, I couldn't get it."

Charles shook his head. "You weren't going about it the right way. I can't believe you didn't realize you've

163

had joint access to his funds all this time. When you told me yesterday you were taking control of his assets, I thought you knew you could have done that at any time."

The realization that she had been unwittingly holding the reins of this monster responsibility jarred her, especially now that Fletcher was not at her side. "Oh, Charles! What am I going to do? What if I do something wrong?"

"Relax. You can always sound out us or Yvonne for advice, and we'll give it to you straight. But I think you've seen enough of the way Fletcher operates to know the right thing to do when the time comes," he said, bending over a plate of drippy pancakes himself.

They ate in silence as Adair thought ahead to her next course of action. Some minutes later, she said, "I want to hire a private investigator to find out who these predators are. I want to find out who hired my father and who shot our helicopter and Harle."

"Okay," said Charles. "You're assuming, of course, that Fletch cannot find that out for himself."

Adair looked up quickly. "No, I'm not assuming that at all. I just want to help him."

"How will a private investigator coming in asking a bunch of questions help him?" Charles asked, holding out his coffee cup for Jackie to refill.

Adair sighed, "You have a point. Then—what should I do?"

"What has he asked you to do?" Charles asked levelly.

Adair looked at the little boy sitting beside her, happily stirring the gooey pancakes around in the plate full of butter and syrup until the mixture attained a uniform texture. She reached over to hug him around the belly, and he stopped his experiment to squeeze her neck and kiss her with sticky lips. "Looks like you've already got that figured out," Charles observed.

He glanced at the wall clock and scooted his chair back from the table. "I've got more meetings this morning with potential buyers. Would you like to come, Adair? You could learn a lot about number crunching."

Just the phrase made Adair wither in distaste. She hated numbers and she would never learn to get along with them. Regarding Daniel, she understood how well Fletcher knew that about her. He had always known that. What was that he said, about making sure before he proposed that she was suitable for the important task he had for her? So where did she ever get the notion that hard numbers were more important than soft souls?

"No," she said, "I'll leave that with you, unless there's something you need to call me about."

Charles studied her over the table. "I'll confess, I couldn't understand at first why Fletch was so convinced you were the one. I wasn't seeing the big picture."

"I look at it this way," Adair said, holding the sticky mess at her side, "Fletcher's got you and Yvonne and the best accountants money can buy to manage his investments, when even a mediocre manager would be better than me. I wasn't even a very good bank teller! But he's got only one person in the whole world to build a bridge between himself and his son, and that's what he chose me for—to help Daniel see that his father is not the monster he's been led to believe. That's my job, and that's what I'm going to do. So I don't get a salary. His whole fortune is at my disposal; what do I need with an office and perks?"

Charles regarded her, then said, "I'll keep you informed on the deals."

"If you think you should," Adair said without concern.

He looked back on his way out of the kitchen. "I don't dare *not*," he replied, and she wondered what he meant.

After Adair and Daniel had gotten all cleaned up, she looked wistfully out at the crisp seventy-degree sunshine. Enduring Dallas's sizzling summers was worth it to have sunny stretches throughout the fall and winter. "I'd like to get Daniel out of the house, but I'm afraid of missing a call," she mused to Alicia, who was getting ready to go to one of her many committee meetings.

"Here." Alicia left the room and came back with a cellular telephone. "Take this. Jackie can ring you if you get any calls here, and she can transfer them to that line. By the way, there's a lovely park and playground just a few blocks from here."

Adair took the telephone. "Alicia, you doll! Thanks! I've passed the park; I know just where it is. We can walk." She paused. "I guess we'll have to, as my car is still in the Streiker garage. I'm afraid to try to go get it. But I'd better decide pretty soon what to do about it and the apartment furnishings."

Thinking about all the dangling loose ends caused Adair to momentarily forget about the park. Straightening her suit jacket, Alicia chided, "There now, you don't. Charles said you have months before anything has to be done, so go on to the park and don't worry over it today. Sometimes if you don't rush these decisions, things fall into place without too much pushing and shoving." She briefly admired her tennis-slim figure in the mirror before blowing Adair a kiss on her way out.

Adair smiled, looking down on Daniel in his sweatshirt and new shoes. "She's right, you know. Well! What say we go play at the park, Dan'l?" He looked dubiously out the window.

With much gentle reassurance, Adair persuaded him to leave bunny and blankie at the house. To prevent Jackie's snatching them up into the washer again, he hid them inside Adair's suitcase in the closet. Then he clutched her hand for their foray out into the jungles of Dallas.

They walked down the block of elegant houses and professionally landscaped yards, then turned a corner and came within sight of the park. Daniel knew what swings were for, and as soon as he saw them he let go of her hand to run ahead. But when a few other children ran up to the swings, Daniel drifted back to Adair's leg.

She was curious to see if he would speak at all to the other children, but knew better than to force him on them. So she set him on the swing farthest from them and began pushing him. He kicked his legs in an effort to swing himself, and mostly just made the swing lurch sideways for his trouble.

The other children, two little girls about five or six, were immediately interested in the handsome boy who had invaded their territory. After trying to pique his interest by ignoring him and finding that unsuccessful, they embarked on a more direct course: they came over to watch him swing. An older woman, possibly a grandmother, sat on a bench some distance away with a book.

"Hello," Adair said, smiling down at the girls as she pushed Daniel. "Do you like to swing?"

"It's okay," shrugged the bigger of the two, a blond girl wearing an appliqued fleece ensemble. "Why are you so brown?" she asked Daniel.

He did not even look at them, as he was watching his new shoes stretch out before him and then disappear under the swing. "Daniel is from Hawaii. He's used to spending most of his time playing in the sunshine, and that makes him brown," Adair answered for him.

The smaller girl shaded her eyes with one hand to look up at Adair. She might have been the sister of the first, and was dressed in an expensive fleece outfit as well. "Are you his mommy?" she asked.

"Yes," Adair said proudly.

"You're not brown," the little girl noted.

"No, but his daddy is. He looks a lot like his daddy," Adair replied.

"Oh." The girls stood watching him a while longer, but as he never looked up they soon got bored and ran off to climb the monkey bars. Adair then rethought her strategy with concern. Daniel would never have any reason to speak if she did all his talking for him.

After a while he'd had enough of swinging and got off to go climb on a geodesic dome. The little girls agreeably came over to join him. The older girl was quite the daredevil, climbing all the way to the top and sitting there. Unaccustomed to his high-tops, Daniel was cautiously making his way around the sides about halfway up.

"Why doncha come up here?" the girl on top challenged. "I can see all around." She put her hands on her hips to demonstrate that she did not have to hold on as she surveyed the park. The smaller girl climbed up almost to the top, then slipped through the bars to swing on one briefly before dropping to the ground. It was a daring maneuver which Daniel made no attempt to emulate.

The younger girl then began climbing up the inside of the dome beneath Daniel. When she had reached the bar Daniel stood on she was hanging almost parallel to the ground. She grinned triumphantly at him through the bars. "Can you do this?"

He declined to try, and began climbing down. His foot slipped on a bar and before Adair could catch him, his chin had thumped painfully on the bar under it.

Adair lifted him off the dome, turning him around to examine the cut on his lower lip. His face screwed up in silent distress and the smaller girl began chanting, "Crybaby, crybaby, run to your mommy."

Adair fished out a tissue for his lip, then walked him over to the spinning platform for a diversion. She showed him how to hold on to a bar and began to slowly spin it. Daniel's reaction of white-knuckled fear caused her to stop it immediately.

Still he stood there, grasping the bar, staring straight ahead. "Daniel?" she whispered in alarm. His unfocused gaze told her something was replaying in his mind. Too late, she realized that the spin might approximate the sensation of a car spinning out of control. His eyes widened in terror and his hands gripped the bar.

"Crybaby, crybaby, run to your mommy!" the girls sang in unison as they jumped onto the platform and started it spinning.

Adair grabbed the bars and halted it with a jerk. She peeled Daniel's fingers off the bar and lifted his stiff body onto her shoulder. As she turned away, the girls followed her taunting, "Crybaby, crybaby, run to your mommy!"

Adair wheeled and put out a hand. Before she said anything, she reminded herself that these children did not know what had happened to Daniel and did not know what they were saying. "Daniel's first mommy died," she blurted. "Don't be mean." She looked over imploringly to the woman on the bench. Immersed in her book, the woman was unaware of anything else.

The girls gazed up at Daniel twisting his fists in Adair's sweater. "That's sad," said the older girl, and the other knuckled an eye. "I'm sorry," said the first, reaching up to pat Daniel's back. Adair lowered him to the ground, but he clung to her neck and would not let go.

"You're not a crybaby. You're a nice boy," said the older girl, patting him on the shoulder. Daniel turned on Adair's shoulder to eye her. "Didja hurt your mouf? Lessee." She bent in matronly concern to look as Daniel stuck out his injured lip for her inspection.

"Poor ting. Lemme kiss it and make it better." The motherly child leaned forward and gave Daniel a sweet little kiss on his lip. She covered her mouth, giggling, as Daniel tried to hide on Adair in an agony of shyness.

"Come pway," insisted the younger girl, taking Daniel's hand. He resisted but Adair pushed him along, following close behind. The older girl took his other hand and they dragged him to the teeter-totters.

The smaller girl clambered up on one side, making room for Daniel on the seat in front of her. After some hesitation, he climbed on. The older girl sat on the other end and Adair stood behind her to help push them up and down.

"My name is Adair. What's yours?" she asked.

"I'm Ashley and that's Lauren and that's our baby-sitter, Ms. Prentiss," the girl replied.

Adair looked far over on the other side of the play-ground, where the woman had not moved from the bench. "I see," she murmured.

Lauren was chattering away at Daniel. As question after question went unanswered, her voice rose in frustration until she complained, "He won't answer me! Why won't he talk? Can't he talk?"

Adair slowly came around to their side of the teeter-totter, leaving Ashley stranded up high. "He's still sad about his mommy, and that makes him not want to talk," she answered.

"Oh. Okay," Lauren said. "That's okay, Dan'l; I'll talk for you." She began carrying on a rather interesting unilateral conversation while Daniel sat in front of her, striving to push up their end of the teeter-totter.

Adair pushed them up and down until they got bored with that and climbed off. The girls took his hands again to run over to the swings, and Adair looked on hopefully to see him clasp their hands and trot between them.

For the next hour or so she silently hovered nearby as they amiably played. It was fascinating to watch them. Daniel never spoke, but having accepted that as the way things were, the girls adapted with remarkable consideration. When there was a disagreement as to whether he or Lauren had reached the high swing first, Ashley took up for the mute Daniel and eloquently argued his case. When he offered Ashley a pretty pebble and Lauren got her feelings hurt, Ashley expressed her conviction that Daniel had another one for Lauren as well. He did, and all was well.

Witnessing all this from nearby on the grass, Adair experienced another of those wonderful epiphanies. What beautiful children, and how satisfying to watch them play. It was a moment of healing which Daniel sorely needed, and all it took was a few words of grown-up explanation, a little nudge in the direction of compassion. Daniel forgot their taunts and his nightmarish flashback; they ignored his speechlessness, and they played as hard as they could under the benign November sky.

But all good things end much too soon; Adair's stomach began growling and Daniel came to lay his head on her shoulder. She looked over to the woman on the bench, who might have been asleep. "When are you supposed to go home for lunch?" she asked Ashley.

"Whenever we want," Ashley shrugged. "We get to do whatever we want."

"That's nice," Adair said. Daniel stretched his arms around her neck and she said, "Well, we had a wonderful time, but we have to go home now. I hope we get to see you here again." She stood with Daniel.

"Okay. Bye-bye, Daniel," Ashley said. Lauren looked up and Daniel opened and closed his fingers in the semblance of a wave.

As Adair carried Daniel across the park, she passed the baby-sitter nodding sleepily on the bench. Shaking her head, Adair glanced back one more time at the girls fifty yards away. Then she paused. They were walking hand in hand toward a wooded creek on the far edge of the park. Beyond that creek was an apartment complex and a major thoroughfare. Two little girls had no business exploring that creek by themselves.

Adair looked at the baby-sitter, who had her eyes closed. "Wait right here," Adair instructed, dropping Daniel to the ground. She began sprinting toward the girls, who were just small dots by now. "Ashley!" she called. "Lauren!"

After Adair had covered half the length of a football field, calling all the while, they finally heard her and turned. She stopped and waved them to her.

When they met her, she panted, "Girls, don't you think it's time to go home now? I do. Let's get Ms. Prentiss to take you home."

Ashley looked longingly toward the creek but Lauren agreed, "I want some Frooty Critters."

"Oh, okay," Ashley relented.

As they turned to walk back, Adair saw Daniel standing frozen where she had left him. She hurried her step, anxious that she might have tapped other fears of abandonment.

But as she drew closer she saw that he was just waiting, just like she had told him to. The look on his face showed nothing more extreme than mild curiosity. Somehow, Adair attributed his healthy reaction to a few good hours of play.

But still he didn't speak, and that disappointed her. *I've got to get him talking to his daddy first*, she realized. *He's going to have to open up to his daddy before he'll talk to anybody else.*

As she walked toward him, she became aware of a car stopped along the curb not far from him. The driver, a man, was watching with more than idle interest. When he saw that he was spotted, he put the car in gear and peeled out.

Adair reached Daniel and swept him up, chills running down her spine. She had to assume they were being watched, that someone with a grudge against Fletcher was looking for an opportunity to snatch Daniel. They were being watched on Paia, in Dallas, and wherever she might choose to run. But after the crash conditioning course of the past few days, this realization did not frighten her as much as remind her to be vigilant.

Ashley tugged on the baby-sitter's arm. "We're ready to go," she told the woman, who yawned and put her book away.

Adair eyed her, then said, "If you don't mind my asking, how much are you paid?"

Ms. Prentiss looked up. "For full-time care, I charge one hundred twenty dollars a week for the first child and sixty for each additional sibling. I do have one opening," she said, smiling at Daniel.

"I see," Adair said. Turning away, she told Daniel, "You can't pay somebody to care." And they walked on back to the Whinnets' house together.

# ~12~

As soon as Jackie opened the door to let in Adair and Daniel, she told Adair, "I got Mr. Whinnet on the line for you, honey. I'm glad you're here, 'cause I was just tryin' to remember how to transfer calls. And *you* look like you could use Jackie's special tuna fish sandwich, mister!" She picked Daniel up in her substantial arms (everyone tended to pick him up) and he looked back anxiously to make sure that Adair followed.

Jackie deposited Daniel in a kitchen chair and Adair picked up the telephone. "Hello?"

"Adair, Chuck here. Listen, we've had an offer to purchase a sizable chunk of the company at what I consider a very attractive price, but I wanted to run it by you for form's sake. Horizons Technologies wants to buy the software company, the data retrieval system, the graphics arts company, and the imaging technology for one point two billion."

"Billion?" she murmured. "Wow—that's a lot of

money. Well, sure, if you think it's a fair price," she said tentatively.

Charles replied, "Yes, I do. Kurtz is waiting in my office now, and—"

"Who?" Adair asked. The name rang a bell.

"Jackson Kurtz, the CEO of Horizons Technologies. I doubt you'd be familiar with the name," Charles replied. "Anyhow, this will dispose of some big headaches for Fletcher and provide him with a nice return on his investment at the same time. So, have I got your okay on that, now?"

Adair did not reply, as she was intently scanning her memory for the context in which she'd heard the name. She knew she had heard it before, and it raised vague apprehensions in her. Why?

Stirring, Adair said, "Uh, wait, Charles. Is Yvonne there?"

"No. She took Sugar to get some office furniture. What's the problem?" Charles asked.

"Well, I'm not sure; only that I want you to wait on that," she said uneasily.

Charles lowered his voice and spoke closer into the receiver. "Adair, this offer is not going to stand while you shop around. Horizons is one of the few acceptable corporations able to make such an offer. It's a take-it-or-leave-it deal, and you've got to make a decision on it right now."

Adair's brows drew together. "Is this Kurtz in the room with you now?"

"Yes," Charles admitted.

"And he knows you're talking to me and not Fletcher?" she asked.

"Yes. I can't explain now, but he had to know," Charles said. "Look, Adair, you said you weren't any good at business and you trusted us to make decisions on matters you knew nothing about. I'm telling you that this is a good deal for Fletcher. If you don't take my advice, I don't know what I'm doing trying to advise you."

He was right, of course, but just as the words of capitulation were about to tumble out of Adair's mouth, a mental picture of her father took shape in front of her eyes. Something about this conversation reminded her of the one with her father last night.

"Give me five minutes. I'll call you back in five minutes," Adair said and quickly hung up. She closed her eyes and bit her lip, trying to dig through her jumbled feelings to find their roots.

It disturbed her that Charles called her in front of this Kurtz person. Since Kurtz must now be aware that Fletcher was out of pocket, and Charles had power of attorney, why should Charles go through the motions of calling her for permission to do something he intended to do anyway? Adair's understanding of the sell-off was that it could take up to two years to do properly. So why was Charles pressuring her to make instant decisions? That just didn't sound like him.

The seconds ticked by as she wrestled with this dilemma, but resolved nothing. She watched Daniel contentedly eating his sandwich, glancing up at her every now and then just to make sure she stayed close by.

Adair melted to watch him. She wondered how many care-givers he had been through, how many hirelings had come and gone, some doing a good job, some doing poorly, but nobody lasting through the year. She empathized with his initial reluctance to let his heart get tangled up with hers. But it is the intrinsic nature of a child to trust; he *had to* allow someone to take care of him because he could not take care of himself.

That being the case, Adair felt the responsibility for his well-being keenly. It is required of stewards that they be found faithful. . . . Adair looked up as Alicia swept into the kitchen from the garage.

"I thought I'd *never* get out of that stuffy room, and on such a beautiful day! I'm so envious that you got to go play in the park. Well? Has Charles called you?" Alicia asked eagerly. She paused to take a finger sandwich from the tray Jackie had prepared.

"Yes; did you know about that?" Adair asked, somewhat surprised.

"All I know is that he and King Kurtz were holed up at the party for *hours* last night, and Charles promised good news after he talked to you today," Alicia chatted.

Adair wanted to know several things at once, but asked, "*King* Kurtz?"

Alicia laughed. "Isn't that mean? It's just a nickname, because some people consider him overbearing—"

Then lightning struck and Adair remembered: a despot. That's what Fletcher had called Kurtz when he was talking on the phone with—Charles. Fletcher had said—what? That he wasn't giving Kurtz a little tiny piece of it, because he made life hell for the people who worked for him.

Adair eyed Alicia. "How much is Kurtz paying Charles to sell him Fletcher's most valuable companies?"

Alicia paled, the hand holding the sandwich falling away. "Kurtz? Paying Charles? What can you possibly mean?"

"What's Charles's new office number?" Adair asked tightly, picking up the phone again. Alicia told her and Adair punched it in.

When Charles came on the line, Adair blurted the uppermost thought in her mind: "It is required of stewards that they be found faithful, Charles!"

"What?" he exclaimed.

"You *knew* Fletcher didn't want to sell anything to Kurtz—I heard him tell you so! So what's your cut for arranging this little deal? You're fired, Charles!" Adair said angrily.

"Adair—," Charles began, but she hung up on him. She was so upset that she was shaking. How tied in was Charles with Kurtz? Was Kurtz one of these predators? And here she and Daniel were staying in the Whinnets' home. She felt like a bundle of raw nerves, exposed and vulnerable.

Adair turned up the stairs to collect her suitcase. Alicia called after her, but Adair did not look behind her until she came to the door of the pink room. Little hands clasped her leg, and she turned to find Daniel right behind her. With tuna smeared in the corners of his mouth, he gazed up at her in mute anxiety.

She knelt to gather him up. "It's all right, Daniel," she whispered. "Mommy just got mad at Uncle Chuck, but not at you. I love you and I'll always keep you with me."

As he gazed at her the anxiety in his face faded. His lips came together to form an *m*. Adair gripped him in expectancy, holding her breath for him to say the word she had applied to herself for the first time.

"Adair." Alicia came up with tears in her eyes. Daniel laid his head on Adair's shoulder without speaking. "Adair, I don't know what the problem is, but please give Charles a chance to explain himself to you. After all the years we've been friends with Fletcher, I just can't imagine Charles intentionally doing anything against his wishes. Please just hear him out."

Adair tried to maintain a stern disposition, but Daniel's nearly speaking had knocked most of the wind out of her, and Alicia's sincere tears finished off the rest.

With a curt nod Adair carried Daniel into the room and sat on the bed. Alicia turned back down the stairs. Daniel scampered to the closet to retrieve his bunny and blankie out of hiding and brought them to the bed where she sat. He then offered her a corner of the blankie. She respectfully declined, so he stuffed it in his mouth and snuggled up against her. In moments he was asleep.

Alicia opened the door. Seeing Daniel asleep, she whispered, "Please come downstairs."

Adair gently removed Daniel's shoes and laid him under the covers. He stirred, so she tucked bunny under his chin and quietly left the room.

She followed Alicia downstairs, where Charles sat at the kitchen table. Adair sat opposite him. For a moment no one said anything.

Then Charles opened his hands. "I'm sorry, Adair. I made a mistake listening to Kurtz. You're right—Fletch had not wanted to sell to him. But I didn't really see Fletch's objections and I thought . . . since you probably were unaware of that—"

"How much did you stand to gain from this sale?" Adair asked.

Charles's clear gray eyes turned flinty. "Not a dime. Not for myself, anyway. But I did get some important concessions from Kurtz to not hamper the rest of the sell-off. And as I tried to explain to you over the phone, Horizons is one of the few corporations willing to take on these concerns and make them run, not just hack them up and resell them. No one will lose their job. The corporation has a good track record with their employees, and *that* was what was most important to Fletcher. He just has this intense personal dislike for Kurtz that seemed to be—well, untenable."

Adair blinked at him and he went on, "Adair, you have to understand how the real world works. Kurtz is in a powerful position, and it's just good business to learn to work deals with people like that, regardless of how much you dislike them personally. Fletch's idealism sometimes gets in the way of his earnings, and I just felt that selling to Horizons was the lesser of two evils, especially since the next highest offer we had for that group was eight hundred million. But this time I was wrong. It was a mistake to disregard Fletch's personal objections. I'd rather be dirt-poor than lose your confidence."

Adair lowered her eyes to the table. The situation was not as bad as she had feared, in that Charles wasn't taking kickbacks. But she was left stinging over the impression that professionally, he still seemed to regard her as a teller.

The doorbell rang, and Jackie silently left the room to answer it. No one in the kitchen spoke while Adair considered her choice of actions. Yes, Fletcher and Charles had been friends for a long time, but as soon as Fletcher was out of the picture, Charles acted contrary to his wishes. Okay, he was genuinely looking out for Fletcher's interests and he admitted his mistake, but Adair's pride still lay in a battered heap.

Jackie reentered the kitchen and stood aside. Someone else entered behind her. Adair glanced up and froze; Alicia gasped and Charles half rose from his seat at the table.

"Hi, gang," Fletcher said mildly, looking from one stricken face to another. "What's going on?" He was dressed in worn denims and an old cotton sweatshirt. His hair covered the stitches on his forehead, but traces of a bruise still circled his left eye.

Dazedly, Adair rose from the table to put her arms

around him. Fletcher kissed her, then drew back with full eyes. He knew they had a lot to talk about.

Charles stood. "Fletch, I cut a deal with Kurtz to buy your technologies group for one point two billion. When I ran it past Adair she got mad—justifiably—because she knew you had been against dealing with him. You . . . may agree that I shouldn't be your manager anymore."

Fletcher glanced at all of them looking to him for his decision. Without batting an eye he said, "I won't second-guess Adair's decisions in my absence. Whatever she said is final."

To underscore that fact, he took Adair out of the kitchen away from the pressure of their presence. But already she was feeling remorseful. "Fletcher . . . maybe I shouldn't have fired him. He believed he was acting in your best interest."

"He blew it. He deserves it," Fletcher replied, glancing around.

"But—one mistake. He admitted it, and it's hard to overlook all the years he's worked for you," Adair argued.

"You can't overlook a mistake that serious," Fletcher said levelly. Then he asked, "Where's Daniel?"

She could not fail to see the irony of the juxtaposition—his referring to Charles' serious mistake, then asking about his own. "He's upstairs, asleep," she whispered. "Fletcher, let Charles keep his job. I think he'll be more careful from now on."

"Are you sure?" he asked skeptically.

"Yes. Yes, of course," she said, aggrieved.

Fletcher thought about it for a moment, then stepped back into the kitchen with Adair on his heels. The Whinnets looked up. "Adair decided this was not a cause for dismissal after all," he told them, and they simultaneously exhaled in relief. Fletcher stood poised, rocking in thought. "One point two billion?" he queried of Chuck, who nodded.

"Tell you what," proposed Fletcher, "offer the board of Horizons to sell them the group for one billion if they will jettison Kurtz."

A sly smile spread on Charles's face. "They'll push him out with a lead parachute." Alicia wiped tears from her face, smiling, and Adair impulsively reached out to hug her.

Then she turned back to Fletcher as if waking up. "What happened to you on Molokai? And how is Harle?" Adair exclaimed.

"He's okay. Harle's going to be okay," Fletcher said hastily. "I know you have a lot of questions, but first . . . do you think Daniel will see me?" he asked in a low voice.

"Let's find out," Adair said. She emerged from the kitchen and started up the stairs with Fletcher behind her.

At that moment Daniel appeared from the upstairs hallway and began sleepily down the stairs, blankie trailing behind him. He saw Adair and Fletcher ascending the stairs the moment they saw him. Adair did not know how Daniel recognized his father, but he did. Daniel went stiff in terror, then with a strangled cry scurried back up the stairs, leaving blankie and bunny stranded on the steps.

Adair looked back at Fletcher in dismay. His parted lips were suddenly flushed and tears welled up in his eyes. "I've never even held him," he whispered. "If he'd just let me hold him. . . ."

Immediately she scooped up the dropped toys and ran after Daniel. Softly calling his name, she opened the door to the pink bedroom and looked around. He was not in bed. She dropped to her knees to look under it, but he was not there.

"Daniel?" she called in a voice barely above a whisper. Opening the closet door, she saw a dress hanging in the back twitch. Adair went to the back of the spacious closet and pushed aside the clothes. Cringing on the floor against the wall was one little boy scared out of his wits.

Adair knelt to lift him up in one knotted burden. He let out another barely human cry and kicked out of her arms to land with a thud on the floor. So Adair lay down on the floor with him and took him in her arms without attempting to lift him. She tucked blankie and bunny under his chin, and he grasped them with little fingers like talons. Then she just lay there and held him on the floor. When he saw that she was not taking him anywhere, he gradually stopped trembling.

Adair held him for a long time before saying anything. Then in a still, quiet voice, she began talking to him: "Daniel, your daddy will not make you see him if you don't want to. He wants to see you very much; he wants to hold you and love you, but as long as you're afraid of him, he won't try to."

She paused, weighing the advisability of what she was going to say next. Whether he would accept it or not depended on how well she had done her job for these last few days. "Daniel, I know your mommy loved you and tried to do the right thing, but she was wrong to keep you away from him. She was wrong to make you think your daddy is a bad man. When you run away from him, it makes him cry. Please, Daniel, give him a chance. You know that I love you. Well, I love him, too. How could I love anybody who would hurt you? I couldn't."

She sat up then, and he allowed her to hold him on her shoulder. Rocking him, she thought about

Fletcher's reaction on the stairs and realized that he would promptly trade that one-billion-dollar group for the opportunity to hold his son like this.

She stroked Daniel's head and he turned his face to her neck. This moment cried out for a comforting song, but Adair did not know any lullabies and "Little Rabbit Foo-Foo" just didn't seem appropriate.

Nonetheless, any mother worth her salt will respond at those times a song is demanded, and Adair finally hit on the right one. In a whisper, she sang: "Jesus loves me, this I know; for the Bible tells me so; Little ones to him belong; they are weak, but he is strong. Yes, Jesus loves me; yes, Jesus loves me; yes, Jesus loves me; the Bible tells me so."

When she stopped singing, Daniel's foot began kicking impatiently, *Go on.* Concentrating to remember the words from years ago, Adair sang, "Jesus loves me, He who died, Heaven's gates to open wide; He will wash away my sin, let his little child come in. . . ."

She sang all four verses, making up words where she was unsure of the originals. And Daniel relaxed until he was a rag doll hanging on her shoulder. Fear was draining, she knew—draining, debilitating, and in the case of his mother, fatal. Now that Fletcher was here, Adair was determined to know all about her, particularly why she was so bent on running from him.

Cautiously, Adair stood and carried Daniel out of the closet. He did not resist. There was a knock on the door. A shudder ran through the little body on her shoulder; Adair held him tighter and said, "Come in."

Alicia leaned into the room. "Fletcher left," she said softly. "He said he'll call you later."

Adair drooped in disappointment. But a moment's reflection told her it had to be this way. She could not force a reconciliation because Fletcher would not force himself on his son. If they were ever to have a relationship, it had to be because Daniel wanted it. "I see," she sighed. "Did he say where he was staying?"

Alicia shook her head. "No."

"Well, did he say anything more about Harle? About what happened in Hawaii?" Adair demanded.

"No," Alicia said, downcast. "He was so—torn up over Daniel that he left right away. He didn't hardly say a word. Charles went back to work as well." Alicia wanted to say more—an apology, reassurance, something—but the right words were hard to come by.

"I understand," Adair said, sparing her the effort. Adair sat wearily on the bed. She tried to be strong for Daniel's sake, but the shock of seeing Fletcher only to have him leave again drained her strength dry. She lowered her head and let the tears come.

Alicia sat on the bed beside her and put an arm around her shoulders. Daniel squeezed Adair's neck tighter and she sat up, stanching the flow of tears. "I'm okay," she smiled weakly at Alicia. "I'd been pretty anxious to see him. But if he said he'd call—I'll just wait, then."

The thought of waiting for Fletcher through another indefinite absence made her weak and nauseous. But the child clinging to her neck caused previously unknown reservoirs of strength to open up.

"Let's see what's going on downstairs," she announced cheerfully, sitting Daniel on the bed to put his shoes back on him.

As Adair finished tying the bright orange laces, Jackie leaned into the room with the phone in hand. "Telephone, Adair. It's Mr. Whinnet," she said, glancing at Alicia.

Adair took the phone. "Hello."

"Adair, Chuck here." The sounds of traffic came

through clearly. "My office just got a call from the investigators we sent to Maui. They're almost certain the fire that destroyed the house you were in was arson. They've taken lab samples to determine what kind of accelerant was used. They'll report back when they get a determination on that."

"I see," Adair said. "Have you told Fletcher this?"

"No, he didn't leave a number with me. He just said he'd touch base later," Charles replied.

"When he does"—Adair pinched the bridge of her nose to keep from crying—"if he calls you before me, please tell him that—that I need to know more about Daniel's mother. I want to know why she wouldn't marry him."

"I'll tell him," Charles said in a low voice, "but frankly, I hope he calls you first."

"Coward," Adair taunted with a weak laugh.

"You said it," he humbly agreed, and Adair was so glad that Fletcher had talked her out of firing him. Although she had not realized it at the time, she was now sure that is what happened.

She handed the phone to Alicia and gathered up Daniel to take him downstairs. In the kitchen, she let him down as Jackie asked her a question about what he liked to eat; then when she turned around again, he was standing at the back door. King Herod was on the other side of the door, whining.

Daniel looked back at her, plainly asking permission to go out. After some hesitation, she opened the door and stepped out into the backyard with him.

King Herod greeted Daniel with many wet, loving kisses and the boy patted him in return. Adair suddenly remembered how the dog had responded to Fletcher in a similar manner. Shaking her head, she thought, *You are your father's son.*

Keeping a wary eye on the dog, Adair walked Daniel around the backyard. There was a swimming pool tucked away in one corner, and the tennis court where Fletcher had landed his helicopter. (She wondered if they'd had to have it resurfaced after that.) The rest of the yard was beautifully landscaped with chrysanthemums, crepe myrtles, hawthorn, and monkey grass, and a pair of sugar maples that glowed a brilliant orange.

Daniel showed interest in the pool but Adair held him firmly back; while hardly doubting that he could swim, she didn't care for either of them to test it out fully clothed. Daniel accepted that the pool was off limits and turned his attention to the pebbles at the edge of the porch. Since he already had a satisfactory collection in his pockets, he concentrated on rearranging them instead.

Adair watched while he industriously carved out roads and rivers, hills and valleys. King Herod crouched at the edge of the activity to watch. Whenever his big nose got too close to the work in progress, Daniel would impatiently push him away. King Herod then sat back and whined.

Daniel created a whole town in the pebbles. He used sticks for trees and buildings, a piece of shingle for a bridge, and leaves for the ocean. He worked in such a focused, deliberate manner that she knew his silence was not due to any lack of comprehension. As a matter of fact, he now seemed to be keenly observant of everything around him. Considering how he soaked up whatever was said in his hearing, Adair began to see how this might be used in building a bridge between him and his father.

After much labor, Daniel stood back and looked at the town he had created. Adair opened her mouth to tell him what a fine town it was when he suddenly jumped in the midst of it and stomped it out of existence. Adair watched in dismay.

Jackie came to the door and said, "Telephone, Adair."

Quickly, Adair hustled Daniel inside and took the phone. "Hello?" she answered breathlessly.

"Yes, is this *Mrs.* Streiker?" The woman's voice was tinged with sarcasm.

"Yes, it is," Adair answered faintly. "Who is this?"

"I had a note here from *Mr.* Streiker asking me to call you," she said, again with that nasty sarcasm. "I am Sandra's mother."

Adair shook her head helplessly. "Excuse me?"

"Oh, didn't he tell you about her? I guess not, huh? My daughter Sandra was his son's mother."

# 13

Adair sat without realizing it. "You're . . . Daniel's grandmother?"

"Technically, yeah, but I want nothing to do with him. I begged Sandra not to go through with the pregnancy, but she wouldn't listen to me. If she had've, she'd be alive today." The woman's voice was steeped in bitterness.

"I'm—so sorry," Adair floundered.

"I'm sorry for you, married to that man. All the money in the world wouldn't tempt me to marry such an evil man. I don't know how he got my phone number, but I see that I'm going to have to change it again."

"Why do you say that?" Adair asked, pained.

"He ruins people's lives. He killed my daughter, my only child," the woman said.

Shaking, Adair said, "Please tell me what happened."

The woman drew a long breath. "My Sandra met him in Hawaii. I don't really know how—first I heard was when she wrote me about this *gorgeous* man she had met. I warned her to find out more about him before she got too involved, but she wouldn't listen. She was in luuuv." The last word was drawn out in irony.

"Then when she got pregnant, what does she do? Of course, she calls her mother. They get in trouble and *then* call the folks for help. She told me who he was then, and that he wanted to marry her. Well, he wasn't inclined to help a poor old woman like *me* out, so I told her to wait until I could do a little research on this man.

"And I did. I started reading all about him in the papers. And I found out that he's a ruthless, heartless, cold-blooded lizard. And I called my Sandra and told her everything I had found out, and begged her to leave him. Well, then she got scared, and she didn't know what to do, because he was pressuring her to marry him.

"But finally I got her out of there—I got her to take as much money as she could get her hands on and leave. And what does that man do? He started chasing her and hounding her. He wouldn't leave her and the baby alone. The more he chased her the scareder she got, and she'd call me, and I'd tell her, 'Run, Sandra! He's going to kill you yet! Mark my words, he won't stop till you're dead and cold.'

"Was I right?" she asked in bitter triumph. "He chased her down on that dark road and she died. He killed her just as surely as if he put a gun to her head. Now my only child is gone and I have nothing. I have nothing," the woman said with a sob.

Adair was silent while the woman cried pitifully. Then Adair quietly asked, "Did he beat her? Did he threaten her? How did he hurt her?"

"What do you mean, how did he hurt her? He killed

her; can't you see that? He chased her down till she died, just like I told her he would!" she cried.

"She took his son," Adair countered. "He wanted to see his son."

"Well, I shoulda known that if you'd marry him, you'd take up for him. I didn't *have* to call, but since he gave me your number I thought to warn you so the same thing wouldn't happen to you as to my precious Sandra, but I can see I'm wasting my breath. Lizards hang together, and all that money is some kind of powerful drug, huh? What I want to know is, does it help you sleep at night? Does it, now? Huh? Huh?" And she hung up with a bang.

Adair slowly put the telephone down. Fletcher could have called her and said, *Daniel's mother wouldn't marry me because her mother poisoned our relationship*, but he didn't. He did something far more effective: let her talk with the sick, poisoned woman herself.

At once other mysteries fell into place, such as the question of why Fletcher chose such an unconventional method of courting her. Adair had to marry him before there was any chance of a physical relationship between them. And before she could form an opinion about him based on all the half-truths and lies circulating about him, he presented her with the bare truth about himself—what all she could handle. She had to admit that had she known *a little* about Sandra and Daniel from the beginning, she might have rejected Fletcher without understanding the whole truth of the matter. That would have made her the loser. Now, she could not imagine life without Fletcher and Daniel, as much as she loved them both. And that made it all the more crucial to see them reconciled.

She turned to Daniel, who was scrunched up on the couch watching her. How much of this could a four-year-old understand? Adair decided to aim high. "Daniel, that was your grandmother. Your first mommy's mother. She . . . is not a nice lady. She made your mommy run from your daddy for no reason at all. He chased her because she took you with her. If she had left you with your daddy, I'm sure he would have let her go and not bothered her. But she had no right to take you away from him. Do you understand, Daniel?"

He shifted on the couch, looked away, then looked back. Adair tried another tack: "Your grandmother does not care about you. She does not care where you are or what happens to you. But your daddy cares, and he always has. He ran after you because he loves you. He's the one who has been providing for you all this time, even when your mommy was running from him. Your daddy did not hurt your mommy, Daniel, and if he had gotten to her before she took off in the car, she would not have died."

Eyes glazed, he sat rocking on the couch. Then he started rocking harder and harder, slamming himself against the back of the couch. Adair reached out to stop him, wondering if she had made a gross error in judgment.

He slid down from the couch and began scampering up the stairs. Adair followed at a distance. She looked into the pink room from the hallway as he went in. A moment later he darted back out carrying something.

Adair followed him back down the stairs. He paused, looking into the kitchen where Jackie was at work on dinner, then he ran to the back door and opened it. Adair stood at the door to watch.

Ignoring King Herod, Daniel dropped the item he was carrying onto the porch. It was his music box. Then he found the biggest rock he could lift, brought it to the porch, and smashed it down on the box. Adair gasped. He brought the rock down again and again until the box was smashed to pieces. Then he sat in a heap and cried furiously.

Adair watched in utter dismay. Was he angry with her for telling him these things? Or with whoever gave him the box? Distressed, she came out to the porch and sat beside him to regard the broken box. He crawled up into her lap for comforting and Adair poured it out, immensely relieved that she had merely opened a festering wound, not inflicted one.

Then she had an idea. Leaving Daniel on the porch, she went back into the kitchen to borrow a large, sturdy spoon. This she took outside and handed to Daniel. Carefully, she gathered up all the pieces of the box and then surveyed the backyard. "Over there," she nodded to a presently bare flower bed.

She and Daniel walked over to the bed, and he looked up at her. "You need to dig a hole," she instructed. Daniel sank to his knees and industriously dug a very fine hole. She placed all the pieces of the music box in the hole and told him, "Now cover it up." He scraped the dirt back over the grave.

Adair fetched a handful of pebbles from around the back porch and began marking out a cross on the grave with them. Daniel brought over some pebbles to encircle the grave. As they worked, Adair murmured, "The box is your mommy's car on that dark road, Daniel. We just buried what happened that night. We put it to rest. You can come back to the grave when you want to think about what happened, but we won't carry it around with us anymore. Okay?"

During the moment Daniel sat on his knees and contemplated that grave, he looked years older than four. But then he stirred restlessly and got up to skip back to the house. Adair wiped the spoon clean of dirt and followed him in.

Daniel ran straight into the kitchen, which smelled wonderfully of cheese and spices. Jackie looked over, pleased at his inquisitive little face. "Do you like pizza, young man?" she asked severely. "I don't mean that phone-in trash. I mean *real* Italian pizza."

"I do," volunteered Adair.

"Well, go wash your hands," Jackie laughed. "We'll eat as soon as it's done."

Adair was directing Daniel to the downstairs half bath when the telephone rang. "Can you get that, honey?" Jackie said in oven mitts.

"Sure," Adair replied, nudging Daniel toward the washroom before she scooped up the phone from the side table. "Hello?"

"Hi, Adair," Fletcher said quietly.

Adair lowered herself to the couch. "Hello, Fletcher."

"Is, uh, Daniel okay?" he asked.

"Yes, he's all right. I talked to him a long time, and he calmed down fine," Adair said.

"Good," he said in a whisper. "Adair, I know . . . you're waiting to hear some explanations. It's just hard to know where to start."

"Sandra's mother called, just like you asked her to. Talking to her cleared up a lot of questions for me," Adair said. The rest of it just burst out: "I still don't understand how people can have such warped opinions about you when they don't even know you—I don't understand it, though I see it so much. But what I really don't understand is how she could possibly not love Daniel. One look at him and you have to love him."

"Do you love him?" Fletcher asked.

"Oh yes, and he knows it. I'm his new mommy," she said.

For a moment Fletcher could not reply. When he said, "Thank you, Adair," his voice cracked. He cleared his throat. "Well, uh, to answer your other questions—"

"Come here to tell me," she said. "I don't want to talk to you over the phone. I want you to come back to the house."

"I don't want to upset Daniel," he said hesitantly.

"Daniel won't see you if he doesn't want to. I'll leave him upstairs when you come," she said, checking out of the corner of her eye to make sure Daniel was listening.

"Well, then—yeah, okay. I'll be by later tonight," he said.

"Okay, Fletcher. Bye," she said, and then turned to where Daniel stood at the foot of the stairs by the washroom door. "Your daddy is coming by tonight because I want to see him. But you don't have to see him. You can stay upstairs while he's here, then after he leaves I'll come get you," Adair told him. He gazed at her.

Adair took his hands, turning them palms up. "Washed your hands yet? Uh-huh, I don't think so. C'mon." She steered him into the half bath where they washed up together.

Following that, Daniel eagerly took his place at the table while Adair set out placemats and napkins. "Where is Alicia?" she asked.

"She had another of them committee meetings. That woman is part of everything that's happening in this town," Jackie said in her usual forthright way.

Adair smiled. "I'm glad she enjoys it. Somebody has to do it. Me, I don't have the temperament for all that society stuff. I'm glad Fletcher doesn't expect that of me. . . ."

She trailed off watching Jackie pull a large pizza pan from the oven. It was the most magnificent pizza Adair had ever seen, so heavily laden with cheese and toppings that Jackie had to use a two-handed grip bringing it out of the oven. "Jackie, that ought to win some kind of award," she said in awe. Daniel was standing on his chair to gaze at it, open mouthed.

"Daniel, have you ever had pizza?" Adair asked. He looked up at her wide-eyed and she answered back, "Even if you have, you've never had one like this, I bet."

The garage door opened and Alicia entered. "What are you cooking, Jackie?" she demanded.

"Saturday night pizza, in honor of Mr. Daniel Streiker," Jackie announced. Daniel clasped his hands in abashed delight.

"Oh, that looks heavenly." Alicia inhaled, standing over it. "Maybe just a tiny piece, Jackie. We have a dinner tonight," she said apologetically to Adair.

"Frankly, I'm glad," Adair said with a smirk. "Fletcher's coming over tonight."

"Is he?" Alicia glanced at Daniel with a smile of restrained excitement. "Oh, I hope it goes well."

"*I'm* looking forward to seeing him," Adair said smugly as she placed a great big piece of steaming pizza on a plate in front of Daniel. He studied it from all angles, then looked up to Adair for help.

"Blow on it until it cools down, then you have to eat it with your fingers," Adair said sternly. Daniel took a huge breath and blew so hard that a few bits of topping jumped across the table. Cackling, Adair corrected, "Blow *easy*, Dan'l. That's all it takes."

She and Jackie sat down with their plates to enjoy pizza with him. And did he ever enjoy it. He dangled the stringy mozzarella and played with the black olives. He did not like the onions, and studiously picked them off, but otherwise devoured that whole great big piece.

Adair was truly amazed and Jackie was gratified.

As they were finishing up, Charles came in. "Good evening, ladies," he said. Adair smiled and he said, "I have to go get ready, but, I thought you'd like to know that I pitched Fletcher's offer to the board of Horizons. They immediately found serious deficiencies in Kurtz's job performance and axed him. It'll probably be in the papers tomorrow or Monday."

"Thank you, Charles," Adair said. He nodded a little awkwardly and left the room.

For dessert, Jackie served up Daniel a bowl of vanilla ice cream, but his little tummy was already so bloated he could hardly eat three bites. He crawled down from the table, went to the video cabinet, and pulled out *The Little Mermaid*. This he presented to Adair in a mute request to put it on. She did, and as it began Daniel curled up on the couch with his blankie and bunny.

Adair helped Jackie clean up the kitchen and put on her coat. "Thank you for dinner. It was fantastic," Adair said.

Jackie shrugged off the compliment. "There's nothing I like better than cooking for kids. They either hate it or love it—you always know where you stand." She went over to the couch and laid a hand on Daniel's head. "Goodnight, Mr. Daniel. See you tomorrow." He looked up, opening and closing his fingers to say goodbye.

Shortly after Jackie left, Charles and Alicia appeared downstairs, ready to go. Adair regarded Alicia's sequined dress with some envy, wondering when she was going to get the opportunity to buy some good-looking clothes for herself. "Have a nice evening. Don't come home too soon," Adair said.

Alicia winked on their way out. "I want to hear every detail when we get back."

Adair grinned, closing the kitchen door behind them. Then she leaned into the television room to say, "I'll be upstairs, Daniel." He raised up from the couch but she did not wait for him as she went up to the pink bedroom herself.

Humming, she checked the stash of spare makeup in the adjoining bathroom and plugged in a set of hot rollers. She glanced up as Daniel's face peeked around the corner of the bathroom. "I have to get ready to see Fletcher tonight," she happily explained.

Chewing on his blankie, he sat in the doorway and watched her apply makeup and roll her hair. Then she opened Alicia's spare closet to look through it. Alicia had offered to let her wear anything she wanted, and just maybe there was something appropriate for the evening Adair had in mind. . . . She knew she had found what she wanted when she spotted a racy denim dress decorated with sequins and snakeskin.

"Excuse me, Daniel," she said as she closed the bathroom door to change. When she emerged to try on a pair of Alicia's heels, even the four-year-old regarded her with masculine appreciation.

Adair checked herself in the mirror one last time and then turned to Daniel, smiling. "Well. I'm going downstairs to wait for Fletcher. Would you like to stay up here or finish watching the movie?"

Daniel got up, indicating he'd go with her. As they left the room she told him, "I'll leave all the lights on for you so that when he gets here, you won't be scared to come up here by yourself." Daniel blinked.

Adair sat with him on the couch to watch the mermaid receive her human legs from the sea witch. Daniel had trouble concentrating on the movie, what with fingering the sequins and beads covering the shoulders of her dress. Adair smiled at him warmly.

The doorbell rang. Adair got up with an expectant smile and turned off the VCR. "That's Fletcher, Daniel. Run upstairs and I'll come get you when he leaves."

He climbed down from the couch and shuffled to the foot of the stairs. Clearly, he was torn. Adair firmly nudged him up to the second step. "Go on, now. He doesn't want to scare you." Then she turned away without waiting to see if he went all the way up.

Adair opened the front door and Fletcher turned around. He looked her up and down. "Hi. You look great," he observed.

"Thank you." She drew him inside for a welcoming kiss. He held her face to kiss her, then slipped his hands down to her waist.

She curled her arms up under his shoulders in such a warm welcome that he was confounded. "I expected some heat, but not this kind," he admitted. "Why aren't you mad at me?"

"I don't feel like being mad," she said as she drew him inside to the TV room. From the corner of her eye she saw Daniel trying to hide on the stairs. Apparently Fletcher did not see him. "Charles and Alicia are gone for the evening and I can't see wasting it being angry," Adair explained. She pushed him down to the sofa and straddled his lap.

Fletcher required no further invitation to help himself to her neck. Adair wrapped her arms around his neck, kissing his head. A curious face peeked around the doorway. Adair smothered a giggle in Fletcher's hair and whispered in his ear.

Fletcher froze, then slowly turned his head as Adair looked up smiling. Daniel stood in the doorway of the television room, blankie in his mouth. "Hello," Fletcher said carefully. Daniel studied him, chewing his blankie.

Adair continued to smile brightly. "Daniel found

some very interesting pebbles outside. Maybe, if you're lucky, he'll show them to you," she said, sliding off his lap.

"I really would like to see them," he confessed. "It's been a long time since I've seen any really nice pebbles."

Adair looked inquiringly to Daniel, but he shied back out of the doorway. Fletcher turned to face forward on the couch, biting back his disappointment.

Adair calmly continued, "Jackie fixed a special Saturday night pizza just for Daniel, and it was great. And we had apple pie with a ton of ice cream on it. I'm not sure whether Daniel liked the ice cream or the pie best—I wish I knew which he liked best," she said, casting a glance at Daniel peeking through the doorway. Fletcher was afraid to turn around and look at him.

"And this morning," Adair continued brightly, "we went to the park down the street, and we met two *really* cute girls. And you know what they thought of Daniel?" She leaned to whisper in Fletcher's ear.

He looked over his shoulder, smiling. Daniel inched forward, driven by curiosity. "Well, of course they liked him. He's my son," Fletcher said proudly. Turning just slightly more toward him: "He's my son, and I'd give anything to have him with me. I'd just give anything if he'd come on over and sit down."

Daniel rocked indecisively in the doorway. Then, with enormous courage, he entered the room and sat on Adair's other side. He leaned under her arm, peering up at Fletcher around her sequins.

Fletcher tried to disguise his shaking hands by clasping them on his knee. He remembered to smile, though, and casually wondered, "So, how 'bout those pebbles you were going to show me?"

Daniel considered it, then stood up to dig his hand

in his pocket. Fletcher hungrily took in every aspect of his appearance, from the big brown eyes to the bright orange shoelaces. Then Daniel withdrew a handful of pebbles and held them out. Fletcher extended his hand, and Daniel dropped five smooth pebbles into his palm.

With restraint, Fletcher closed his hand over just the pebbles and held them while he looked at Daniel. Scratching his brow, Fletcher opened his hand again to study them. "These are very nice," he admitted seriously, glancing up. "They're very smooth, and not all of them are brown. This one has some black spots and this one is half white," he remarked, placing them on the coffee table one at a time. "They're all so nice, I don't know which one I like best. Which one do you like best?" he asked Daniel.

With brows drawn tight in consideration, Daniel leaned over the pebbles. He was now standing right beside his father, who was visibly fighting the urge to touch him. At length Daniel chose a brown pebble with a blue streak, and presented that to Fletcher. "Is this one mine?" Fletcher asked, taking it from the little hand. Daniel regarded him silently and Fletcher said, "Thank you."

Tentatively, he held his arms open to the boy. Daniel fidgeted uncertainly beside Adair. Then he climbed up on Fletcher's knee. The father closed his arms over his son and rocked him. "Thank you," he repeated, looking up at Adair with red eyes.

Daniel turned in Fletcher's arms and reached out to Adair. She leaned forward so he could grasp her around the neck. Thinking that Daniel wanted to go to her, Fletcher let go of him. But Daniel still held his neck as he pulled her forward. He brought them face to face to make them kiss, then watched up close in satisfaction. Choking back a laugh, Adair planted her mouth on Fletcher's for a good wet one.

He kissed her and sighed, leaning his head against Daniel's chest. Suddenly he looked up and exclaimed, "Come with me. Tonight. Both of you."

"What?" said Adair.

"I have to go back to Hawaii to wrap up some loose ends. I was intending to go by myself, but—I want you and Daniel to come with me. You'll get a front-row seat to the action," he said.

Adair looked at Daniel in excitement. "What say, Dan'l? Want to fly on that nice plane back to Hawaii?" He scampered down off Fletcher's knee and ran up the stairs.

Fletcher drooped. "He's running to hide, isn't he? I asked too much, too soon. I shouldn't have pushed so hard."

Adair did not know what to say. But a few moments later they heard little footsteps descending the stairs, and Daniel appeared with his nylon bag all packed.

Beaming, Adair turned to Fletcher. "We're ready to go!"

# 14

While Fletcher called a cab, Adair left a note for Alicia, thanking her for her hospitality and promising her restitution for the dress and shoes she was borrowing. When Fletcher found out those were Alicia's things she wore, he gave her a wad of hundred-dollar bills to leave with the note. Then the cab pulled up and they piled in the back seat, Fletcher directing the driver to Love Field.

Riding in the dark cab, Adair looked across at Fletcher and down at Daniel between them. Fletcher's eyes went from her to his son. Daniel was sitting contentedly, straightening every now and then to see what some interesting lights belonged to. Fletcher caressed her shoulder. "He—looks good," he murmured. "You say he's been eating?"

"Like a pig," she answered. "Why?"

"They told me he . . . wouldn't eat much. He'd go for long stretches without eating," Fletcher answered painfully. Adair shook her head. "And no head-banging?" he asked.

"What?" Adair said.

"He hasn't been banging his head on things?" Fletcher asked.

"Heavens, no. That would hurt," she said in offense.

Fletcher ran a hand over his mouth and glanced out the window. "I don't know how you did it, but I'll never be able to thank you enough," he said quietly. "Has he talked to you?"

"No," she said in disappointment. "Not a word."

He nodded, placing a light hand on Daniel's head. The boy looked up at him without a trace of fear and Fletcher turned to the window, blinking rapidly.

The cab delivered them to the section of the airport which Adair had seen before, and they climbed on the cart that would take them to Fletcher's jet. Adair held Daniel firmly on her lap, but he still bounced up and down with excitement to ride on the cart. It was better than an amusement-park ride. Chirruping, Daniel pointed at the runway lights stretching out over a distance.

"What did he say?" Fletcher quickly leaned over.

"He just laughed," Adair shook her head. "Patience, Daddy." She smiled.

"Yeah," he said, nodding and gripping her hand.

The cart pulled right up to the steps of the plane and they boarded. Daniel bounded all around its sleek interior before Adair caught him and strapped him in a seat. By the time they took off, he was sound asleep.

When they reached cruising altitude, Fletcher got up to recline Daniel's seat, leaving him strapped in.

Adair stretched out on the sleeper and kicked off the borrowed heels (Alicia's feet being a half size smaller than her own). Fletcher climbed onto the bed beside her and lay back.

"Now you can tell me what happened on Molokai," she informed him.

"Yeah." He touched his stitches. "A farmer on the island saw our chopper go down and picked me up in his truck after you had left. I was out of it for a day and a half—still got a monster headache—and by the time I came 'round enough to know what was going on, you had jumped the islands with Daniel, and Harle had gotten himself shot trying to find me. I had to hustle."

"You found time to call Longview yesterday," she noted.

He inhaled. "That was a matter of taking care of the simplest things first—and finding out whether you had called your parents when you got stateside."

"Did Charles tell you the investigators found it was arson?" she asked, jumping to the event that drove her back to Texas.

He regarded her. "Yeah. You kept a cool head and showed some real initiative. I appreciate that."

She blushed. "I had the crazy idea of taking over your assets, since you were missing."

"Why is that crazy?" he asked, propping himself up on an elbow. "I set it up so you could, in the event of just such an occurrence."

She grew embarrassed. "I'm not capable of handling that much responsibility. I mean—firing Charles—" She rolled her eyes.

"Hey—he's an employee. You're my *wife*," he said emphatically. "It worked out okay that you changed your mind, but even if you hadn't, I'd have backed you. I wanted Chuck to understand that he's not to take you lightly."

"Thanks," she whispered gratefully, "but there's a lot more I have to learn before I could handle things the way you do."

"Not as much as you think," he remarked, glancing over at the sleeping Daniel. Adair looked too, and the sight of him resting peacefully in Fletcher's presence thrilled her.

"Now," Fletcher murmured, toying with her zipper, "let's check out this dress."

"What about your headache?" she asked with concern.

"What headache?" he returned, hiking up the shirred skirt.

⌒

**H**ours later, after they had arrived at Honolulu International, Adair was awakened by masculine voices. She sat up sleepily to see Fletcher standing near the cockpit discussing something with two other men, and in her disoriented state she thought she heard the word *raid.* "What?" she mumbled.

Fletcher nodded to the men and came over to zip her dress decently. "Ready to go home?" he asked.

"Um-hmm." She stretched, then watched as he turned to unstrap Daniel from his seat. Lovingly, he lifted the limp body to his shoulder and reached a hand toward her. Adair followed them out, pausing to pick up the dropped blankie and the nylon bag.

*What a beautiful night.* Adair sighed, pulling windblown hair from her face. Shouldn't she be afraid, coming back here in the middle of the storm? Not when she was with Fletcher and Daniel. Seeing them finally together made her feel that whatever else happened would merely be the denouement.

They crossed the stretch of asphalt toward oncoming headlights. Fletcher stopped as his Porsche pulled up to them. Spud hopped out, leaving the engine idling. "Howzit, Bosslady?" he asked amiably.

"Fine, Spud," she said. "I called Spud to pick us up on Maui and take us to Dallas," she told Fletcher.

"I know," he replied, grinning back at her. He looked so happy carrying the little form on his shoulder.

"We gotta talk story, Boss," Spud said, leaning on the car as Fletcher laid Daniel in the back seat and strapped the seat belt around him.

"Tomorrow at one. You tell the crew to meet me at Ono, and we'll talk plenty," Fletcher said ominously. He glanced over at Adair settling in the front seat.

"*Shaka*, Boss." Spud grinned in anticipation, holding up the thumb and little finger of one hand. "Laydahs." He pointed as Fletcher sat and put the car in gear. With a wave to Spud, they took off.

"What's that?" she asked. "What do you have to meet about?"

The car lurched slightly as Fletcher shifted gears. "I guess I should tell you why I was coming back—to break some faces for that little inconvenience at the Lokomaikais' house. I was trying to be patient and play it cool, but these predators have gotten on my nerves. This little killdeer has decided to sprout claws."

"Who's doing all this? Do you know?" she asked anxiously.

"No, but it doesn't matter. I know where they are," he replied.

"Where?" she asked.

"At an estate on the big island. They did something really stupid to give themselves away," he said, scanning around them as he stopped for a red light.

"What?" she asked.

"They kidnapped Harle right out of the hospital for a ten-million-dollar ransom. Of course, the bodyguard that I had put over him saw it all, and tracked them to the big island."

"Is Harle all right?" she asked.

"Oh yeah; they won't damage the bait. But we're going to spring him," he said grimly.

Adair checked Daniel sleeping soundly in the back seat. "I don't understand . . . after trying to burn down the house around me and Daniel, and shooting Harle, why are they holding him for ransom?"

He glanced over. "The idea wasn't to kill you, Adair; it was to kidnap you. The arson was just a diversion. Bad idea. I understand you were a little too alert and slipped away before they could grab you. Harle got shot because he got in the way. But he's such a valuable employee they decided he'd do to lure me back to the nest. The idea has always been to get to me through the people closest to me."

"So—you're going to raid the estate to get him out," she said.

"Yep," he confirmed, whipping the car around a corner.

"When will I find out how it went?" she asked dismally.

"You'll see it for yourself," he said. "I'm taking you with me. Daniel, too."

"You're—Fletcher, you're kidding!" she exclaimed.

"Not in the least. You'll be absolutely safe, and I thought you'd get some satisfaction from seeing it come off," he said.

"Would I!" she echoed, and he smiled.

They were silent for the next several minutes as Adair envisioned black-garbed commandoes rolling out

of doorways amid machine-gun fire. But then she realized that if it were going to be like that, he would never
allow his wife and four-year-old son to tag along. Still,
it had to be worth watching. And she entertained
absolutely no doubts that he would accomplish exactly
what he intended.

"Fletcher," she remembered, "my father showed up
at the Whinnets' last night. My first father, Carl."

He nodded. "Chuck told me about that."

"I don't think Charles knew that he also came to
your house here. Remember when we were in the sunroom and Nona answered the door—we heard them
talking over the intercom?" she asked.

"Yes," he said.

"I knew I recognized the voice—that was Carl!
Somebody's bankrolling his travel. He told me his business had gone bust," Adair said with some shame.

"Okay," he acknowledged softly. "Don't worry about
it."

Adair took him at his word, watching the myriad
lights retreat below them as Fletcher began the drive
up Tantalus through a tropical wonderland. He slowed
on the curves, and Adair caught exotic fragrances mingling in the night air. She felt their welcoming embrace
was meant for her—all at once this place was hers, just
like Daniel had become hers.

"Fletcher, I want to live here. I want to live in the
house you already have here," she said.

"It's yours," he said, pulling down the long drive
to the gate. He opened it with the code, then drove on
up to the house and parked.

Adair got out and leaned down to unstrap Daniel,
but Fletcher said, "Please let me get him." So she stood
back for him to lift his son onto his shoulder, then
handed him the requisite blankie.

209

Since Nona was not here, Fletcher opened the front door with a key on the ring with the car keys and Adair led the way to the winding stairway. They ascended, then she watched from the doorway while Fletcher put Daniel to bed in the room across the hall from theirs.

He came out, closing the door partway. "I'll be to bed soon," he whispered, touching her face.

"I'll wait," she promised. He went downstairs while Adair slipped off the dress and climbed under the sheets. But as soon as her head hit the pillow, she was out.

A jostling of the bed woke her. Adair lazily reached over and felt a bony knee. She uttered a breathy chuckle, whispering, "Hi, Daniel. Did you get lonely?" She looked up at the boy sitting beside her, chewing on his blankie. On his other side Fletcher lay snoring softly.

Adair lifted herself on her elbow, pulling up the sheet. It looked to be the middle of the night, but she was wide awake. And from the way Daniel was working his blankie, he seemed ready for breakfast. So Adair slipped off the bed and tiptoed to the wardrobe for a muumuu.

Once dressed, she came back to the bed and held out her hand to Daniel, who scampered down to take it. Then they took themselves downstairs.

Adair clicked on a light and looked around the bright tiled kitchen. Tall green giants swayed gently just outside the large windows as if asking to come in. Daniel hopped onto a chair at the rattan-and-glass table in the sunroom and looked up expectantly. "Oh, dear. I don't know how to make *poi* yet," Adair muttered, opening the refrigerator.

Ah. There was milk. Adair opened a cabinet and

found a box of Chirpy-O's. "Dan'l, I'm going to fix you a good, old-fashioned Dallas breakfast to welcome you to your new home in Honolulu," she declared, pouring a bowl of cold cereal. For tropical flavor, she sliced up a banana in it. That was good enough for Daniel; he took the spoon she held out and dug in.

"What's going on?" Fletcher, grizzled and grumpy, stood at the foot of the stairs in his underwear. "Do you people know that it's four o'clock in the morning?" he asked gruffly. Daniel lowered the spoon, debating whether to be scared or not.

Seeing that, Fletcher softened right away. He came over and knelt by Daniel's chair, placing a hand on his tummy. "Just asking. We'll move up sunrise if you like." Daniel considered that, then returned to his cereal.

Fletcher pulled up a chair next to him. "Man, that looks *ono*. Could I have a bowl of that, please?" he inquired of Adair. She smiled to herself as she fixed him a bowl of Chirpy-O's just like Daniel's.

He received it with thanks, then propped his elbows on the table to eat with Daniel. He held the spoon in his fist like Daniel did, eying him sidewise as he ate. Whenever Daniel looked over Fletcher would avert his eyes, but then look back when he thought Daniel wasn't looking. Daniel then started trying to catch him, and would look up unexpectedly. There were many feints and near misses, then Daniel wheeled around just as Fletcher glanced over, and he was caught.

Daniel cackled in victory, standing in the chair to plant his hands on Fletcher's face to make him look him in the eye. "You got me," his dad laughed. "I give."

Adair stood watching. Did Daniel understand that he had caught the fearsome bogeyman, the monster whom he'd dreaded meeting all his short life? Did he realize that this monster was really someone who could

211

just about call up an early sunrise for his son's pleasure?

Daniel sat back down and continued eating companionably. Fletcher finished his cereal and pushed away the empty bowl. "We'd better go back to bed, or we'll never make it through the day. It's gonna be a full one," he said.

Adair nodded. "You go on; we'll be up in just a minute." Fletcher hesitated. "We'll be right up," she promised. So he scooted his chair back and stood. He wanted to linger with Daniel, but evidently decided not to push it and went on up the stairs.

While Adair washed out the bowls in the sink, Daniel pressed his face against the glass walls of the sunroom. He knew he was home in Hawaii, but he did not know where this particular place was, and he was anxious to explore. The darkness outside did not appear to daunt him, but it did Adair, who was not about to let him out.

In a few minutes she turned out the lights and led him back up the winding staircase. For form's sake, she attempted to tuck Daniel back in the bed across the hall, but he would have none of that. He beat her back to her own bed, where Fletcher made room for them both.

When Adair woke for the second time that morning, she felt so leaden and groggy that she regretted going back to sleep. There was no one else in her bed, and the bed across the hall was empty as well. With a curiosity bordering on concern, she trotted down the stairs to look around.

There was a carpeted room on the other side of the kitchen which had a pool table and one wall covered with bookshelves. Fletcher, shaved and dressed, was sitting in a leather recliner with Daniel in his lap, reading to him. Adair paused at the door to absorb the sight.

Fletcher looked up, leaning his head back on the headrest. "Good morning," she smiled.

He lifted the book, a photograph album. "I was explaining to Daniel where he got his name. He never knew his grandfather," he said with a note of regret.

Adair wondered, "If Sandra wouldn't even let you see him, how did you ever get her to name him after your father?"

"She didn't know that was my father's name," Fletcher answered, glancing away. "She thought she was spiting me. She had another boyfriend named Daniel."

"I see," she said quietly, coming to sit on the arm of the recliner. Daniel reached out a little hand to twine in her muumuu. "Did your parents know about him?" she asked as she held Daniel's hand.

Fletcher shook his head. "Neither did Desirée, until recently. I told her about him right before I—we—left Dallas for Mom's funeral. I think that's one reason she was so upset when I called from Honolulu," he reflected. "So. Are you ready? We're due there in thirty minutes."

"Ready?" she startled. "Due at Desirée's house? No! I just got up!"

"Well, you'd better hurry, then," he said, holding the album steady for Daniel to turn the page.

Adair muttered indignant words as she hurried upstairs, though she knew she was not angry, only nervous.

She got herself ready within the prescribed thirty minutes, then came down to check on Daniel. Fletcher had him dressed in a bright aloha shirt and shorts, and of course, the beloved bulky high-tops. With deadly seriousness he attended to Fletcher's demonstration of how to tie the laces. Adair looked on, biting her lip to keep from laughing.

After a quick breakfast of island fruit and more Chirpy-O's, they took off in Fletcher's Porsche. Adair was not a reliable judge of model years, but this one looked to be very new. "You told me you didn't have a car," she remarked.

"Not in Dallas—you couldn't pay me to drive there. But here, I like to drive," he responded.

*Fast*, she noted inwardly, gripping the armrest and looking back at Daniel, who was holding up his blankie to watch it stream in the wind.

Adair turned back to Fletcher. "Are we going to be late?"

"No. She doesn't know we're coming," he said.

Adair floundered, "She doesn't! I thought you said—"

"I said we were due there, but that was by my timetable. I haven't called Desirée to tell her that," he replied.

"Oh, boy," Adair murmured apprehensively. Growing thoughtful, she asked him, "Fletcher, if neither Desirée nor your parents knew about Daniel, where was he raised?"

"All over the islands. Sandra could jump from island to island without leaving a trail and disappear inland somewhere. It was really hard to find her, sometimes. And sometimes when I did find her, I'd leave her alone for a while, not try to contact her. But I'd slip up and watch Daniel whenever she took him outside to play. Once, when they were on Kauai, she left Daniel out by himself and he wandered over to an irrigation ditch and fell in. Do you remember that, Daniel?"

Fletcher twisted in the seat to look at the boy. "Do you remember the man who came running and fished you out? And then your mom screaming and him running away?" Daniel gathered his blankie protectively under his chin.

"That was me," Fletcher said. "That was the only time before yesterday that I'd even seen him up close. Oh, man—I wanted to just grab him up and run."

"Why didn't you?" Adair asked pensively.

He shook his head. "It was a temptation, for sure. But—it wouldn't have been right. It wouldn't have been good for Daniel. I wanted him to *want* to know me, but by the time Sandra . . . went away, I couldn't even approach him. I needed a go-between. You had every right to be upset that I didn't explain all this to you beforehand, but, I wanted you to *see* him first—to—to see how much he needed you, and how much he meant to me. . . ."

Adair nodded. "Is this part of the reason you didn't tell Desirée we were coming?"

He glanced at her guiltily. "Getting predictable, am I?"

"I wish," she replied in mild disgust.

"As a matter of fact, there's more I need to tell you, but . . . right now is not a good time," he said, glancing back at Daniel.

Adair could hardly imagine what else he had to spring on her.

A few minutes later Fletcher turned off past the University of Hawaii campus down a shaded suburban avenue. He turned another corner and pulled up to a plantation-style house with banana trees in front. Evaluating the house, Adair decided that Fletcher took good care of his sister.

He parked and hopped out, clapping and opening his hands toward Daniel. The boy had his seat belt unbuckled in an instant, standing up on the seat to launch himself into his daddy's arms. As Adair followed them up the walk to the house, Daniel looked over his dad's shoulder to make sure she was right behind them.

Fletcher took the steps two at a time up to the front door and rang the bell. Adair stood beside him. Daniel reached out to her face and she kissed his little palm.

The heavy front door opened, and they looked down at a young girl in a Sunday dress. "Hi, Charity," Fletcher said easily. "I want you to meet your Aunt Adair and your cousin Daniel."

The little girl gazed up at Fletcher with heavily fringed brown eyes. "Mom!" she called in a warning tone. "Mom, I think you better come to the door!"

A moment later a lovely, childlike woman with softly curling brown hair and deep brown eyes like Fletcher's came up behind the girl, staring. Adair observed that apart from the eyes and complexion, brother and sister looked not much alike.

Desirée's gaze went to Daniel's face, then Adair's; then she stepped back and said, "Come in."

Carrying Daniel on one arm, Fletcher observed, "Not as many press corps out today, so I thought we'd stop by. Desirée, meet my family: Adair and Daniel."

Mustering a smile, Desirée offered a hand to Adair. "Hello."

"The painting you sent is lovely. I'm going to bring it down to our house here," Adair said happily.

"You're going to be living here?" Desirée asked faintly.

A big, good-looking Caucasian man came up behind her. "Fletcher," he grinned, sticking out his hand. "Good to see you."

"Howzit, Clay. This is my lady Adair," Fletcher said warmly. Adair shook his proffered hand, but was still distracted by Desirée's stricken face.

"And this—," Fletcher began, hoisting Daniel.

But Desirée interrupted him: "Fletcher—come to the other room for a minute, please."

"Why, Desirée?" Fletcher asked. "Something bothering you?"

His sister looked away in distress. Her husband stood back with patiently folded hands and a look that said, *Great. Here it comes.* Adair tried to smile at Charity while telling herself that Fletcher had everything under control. "Why are you doing this, Fletcher?" Desirée asked.

"I thought you'd want to meet my family," he said.

"Not that. I mean—why must you make such a . . . a scene? You turned mother's funeral into a circus!" she said in a restrained voice.

"Just because I thought Aunt Margot deserved a little familial support, like the minister said?" Fletcher asked innocently. Clay's face betrayed a grin before he caught his wife's glare and sobered.

Fletcher added, "Would you be interested to know that the minister who stepped in for Father Cho works for a competitor of mine in Dallas? Would you care to know how much that 'minister' pulls down a year?"

"No," she said stonily.

"Or that he's the one who fed information about the funeral to the press? Where do you suppose they got the photos of her lying in the casket?" Fletcher pressed.

"Stop it!" Desirée cried. "Fletcher, just stop it! I—don't know who you are anymore. I don't understand you."

"Why? Because I wouldn't finance your friends' ventures? Because I won't do everything you ask me to?" Fletcher asked coolly.

Her pretty face screwed into a miserable pout. "You had no good reason for turning them down. You made me look like a liar."

"You should know not to try to set my agenda for me, Desirée. I love you, and I'll always be your safety net, but nobody pulls my strings," Fletcher said.

She shot a quick look at Daniel in his arms. "Looks like *somebody* has," she returned. Adair cringed.

Fletcher squeezed Daniel. "You're right. Two some-bodies have. They sneaked in and displaced you as my primary family. Adair weaseled her way in by loving me enough to do whatever I asked, and Daniel did it by sheer need—not to mention that he was mine to begin with. I'm sorry that I embarrass you, Desirée, but the fact is that you just don't have all the information that I do. If you're going to be my sister, you're going to have to turn a deaf ear to all the gossip and criticism because I will not explain myself, defend myself, or change my agenda to suit you or them. Anybody who's really interested in what I've done can look at the pub-lic records and draw their own conclusions about me. Everybody else can just—go their own way." He said all this in a calm, loving tone.

Desirée looked at the floor and her daughter leaned comfortingly against her hip. Fletcher turned back to the door. "You've got my number. Call me when it's a better time for us to come visit," he said. Then he took Adair and Daniel out to his car and they departed.

# ~15~

letcher took his family out for lunch to a no-frills, neo-sixties' restaurant. Adair recognized it at once as a locals' haven due to the lack of touristy glitz and the abundance of pidgin.

As soon as they were seated at a Formica-topped table, Fletcher tossed aside the menu and ordered several dishes, the mention of which caused Daniel to start bouncing in anticipation. Adair studied the menu to try to figure out what he was ordering; when she saw how much *opihi* cost—the raw limpets which she had earlier disdained—she resolved to try them this time.

When their dinner arrived, Daniel sat on his knees to be able to reach all the dishes with his fingers. Adair restrained him, urging a fork on him. She glanced up for support from Fletcher, who merely smiled. "Well, I can tell you're going to be a big lotta help with the discipline," she cracked.

"There'll be plenty of time for discipline. Right now

I just want to watch him enjoy himself," he said. He glanced up and made eye contact with a burly native who strolled on past.

Over the next thirty minutes Adair observed several people come in who discreetly caught Fletcher's eye and then walked past him to a back room. When Spud entered in this manner, Adair knew the meeting was at hand.

Fletcher stood, tossing a large bill on the table. He nodded Adair toward the back room but Daniel, with his messy hands, started the dance of physical necessity. "Let me take him to the restroom and we'll meet you," she whispered. Fletcher grinned down at Daniel and Adair steered him toward the opposite corner. She paused before two doors, one marked "*Kane*" and one marked "*Wahine.*"

Daniel looked up at her impatiently and then pushed through the *kane* door. A man came out of the restroom as Daniel went in, so Adair had no choice but to wait in the corridor holding his blankie. An uncomfortably long time later Daniel emerged and triumphantly presented his palms, which smelled of soap. Adair kissed the sweet little hands and Daniel reclaimed the blankie.

They went through the back door after the others. Fletcher was sitting on the edge of a desk in the office/storage room, presiding over a group of about twenty. A few looked over as she and Daniel came in, and Fletcher gestured her to the chair behind the desk. Daniel chose to stand on the desk and hang on Fletcher's shoulders, which he encouraged.

One man was in the midst of reporting: "The estate

covers about fifty acres in the Kau district. It's owned by the Warfield Group out of New York City. [Fletcher's chin came up in recognition.] On the western edge, near Manuka State Park, there are condominiums and a private conference center. But we don't think Harle's being kept there—the signs are that he's in a house south of there, on the edge of the desert. There's also a large marijuana field on the estate," he remarked.

Adair stood to look over Fletcher's shoulder at the photographs handed him. They were aerial views of a ramshackle frame house surrounded by a decaying wood fence and dry, windswept grassland, followed by neat rows of tall cannabis plants.

Fletcher cocked his head to study the photos while Daniel hung on his neck. Adair considered trying to pry him loose, but Fletcher did not seem to object to his interference. Remembering what he had told Brian about being his daddy's "tick," she knew this was a long-desired nuisance.

"Is it guarded?" Fletcher asked.

"Somebody's out front all the time with a carbine—sometimes there are two of them," the reconnaissance man replied.

"Uh-huh. Have you actually spotted Harle there?" Fletcher asked.

"No," the man shook his head. "We haven't actually seen him there at all. Bernie traced him by the locals' reports of them carrying an injured man in on a stretcher. By the description, we're sure it's Harle," the reconnaissance man explained.

"Let's see the condos," Fletcher said. He was handed other pictures of a crescent-shaped building. As he looked these over, he asked, "So what's the complication?" referring to something Adair had missed while waiting for Daniel.

The reconnaissance man looked reluctantly at somebody else, then replied, "There's a lot of comings and goings at the condos, especially at night. Looks like reinforcements—eleven guys at last count. We think . . . they're expecting you."

"You think they're gearing up for an attempt to rescue Harle?" Fletcher asked.

"Yes sir, that's exactly what we think. It looks like a setup, with bait and trap," the reconnaissance man said with certainty.

Thinking, Fletcher leaned his head back on Daniel. The boy planted a smooch on his cheek and Fletcher briefly closed his eyes. Adair asked timidly, "If this is a trap, why the ten-million ransom demand?"

The reconnaissance man looked at her to reply, "We believe that's a smoke-screen to cover up their true intent. They're not nearly so interested in getting the money as they are the man." So saying, he nodded toward Fletcher.

"About a year ago, there was a doctor on staff at Kona Hospital who suddenly left his practice there, and then surfaced a few months later in a Dallas clinic owned by the Warfield Group," Fletcher said abruptly. "What was his name . . . ? Aston."

No one else remembered, so no one said anything; but Fletcher had answered his own question. His hands reached up to the small arms clasped around his neck, and a strained expression came over his face, as if he were deliberating the hardest choice he ever had to make.

Then his face smoothed and he said, "Well, if they're expecting me, it would be rude to not show. But we don't have to give them any more time to get ready." He returned to the pictures, studying them minutely. "Tommy, tell me what you've seen at these condos."

Another man in a T-shirt featuring Lieutenant Worf

shifted and said, "They're empty right now, being cleaned for a convention coming up in December."

"Who's cleaning them?" Fletcher asked.

"Some locals from Waiohinu," Tommy replied.

"Who?" asked Fletcher.

Tommy pointed to the reconnaissance man. "Sergio talked to one of the maids."

Fletcher turned expectantly to Sergio, who shrugged. "She didn't know anything. Hadn't seen anything."

Fletcher inhaled impatiently. "Did they clean *every* unit?"

"Ah, she said they were paid to clean twenty, but only had to do nineteen. The last unit was being painted," Sergio said.

"And you saw the painters go in and out. You saw tarps and paint cans," Fletcher said.

"Well, no, we didn't see any of that. It was closed up the whole time," Sergio admitted.

"Which unit?" Fletcher asked, looking at the pictures. Sergio came over and pointed it out. Fletcher nodded. "The house is an ideal site for a trap, but the condo is a better place to hide a wounded man."

"That's a top-floor unit. If he *is* there, it'd be tough to get to him." Sergio pointed it out on the photo.

"But it's got a flat roof," Fletcher observed, turning the photo. "Okay," he said with finality. "Tommy, you, Blaine, and Hove take a cage in the Goose. You land here on the roof and go in the unit through the window. Meanwhile, Sergio and I'll buzz the house in the Blackbird to get their attention. You wait for my signal to land. Spud, you and Jeeter will hover out of sight in the Pelican, to assist if one of us gets in trouble. Questions?"

"They're armed, Bossman," Spud remarked. "So what do we use?"

"No one's getting shot," Fletcher said testily. "The moment we hit the area, we drop the stun grenades and the pepper mace grenades. Blaine and Hove will take the stun guns and the pepper mace when they go in for Harle—be sure to take an extra gas mask for him. No one's to fire live ammunition without my go-ahead. Any other questions?" That seemed to settle it, so he said, "Let's go."

As he stood the group began filing out of the room. Fletcher turned back to Adair and said, "I'm sure you understand why I can't take you and Daniel, after all. But one thing I can do is set up communication between us." Gesturing to one young guy nearby, Fletcher instructed, "Go get that shortwave radio and set it up for Adair, here."

"Yes sir." The guy flashed out the door.

Fletcher gently disengaged Daniel's grip on his neck as he told Adair, "You'll be able to hear all communications between choppers, and be able to talk to me if you need to. And Daniel," Fletcher turned to look him in the face. He struggled with what to say that a four-year-old could endure to hear. "Your dad loves you, Daniel. Please remember that I'm the one who fished you out of that irrigation ditch, okay?"

Daniel looked at him. Fletcher reached over to kiss Adair, and in so doing transferred Daniel to her arms. "You're not going to get hurt, are you?" she asked.

His eyes rested on Daniel. "I suppose that's up to you, kid," he mused, then answered Adair, "Of course not. I never get hurt." Adair eyed the stitches on his forehead. Then with a brief pat on Daniel's back he was gone.

Adair sat Daniel on the edge of the desk and paced in front of it while Daniel drummed his heels on the desk. What was this about the Warfield Group? And the doctor who had joined them? A trap?

Before she got too far along in working up a monumental state of anxiety, she remembered his telling Desirée that she didn't understand him because she didn't have all the information he had. Adair had certainly come to respect his network of contacts. And as the brain, he was able to put together pieces that were incomprehensible to everyone else. Harle had said that he always knew what he was doing. Choosing to believe that now, Adair sat behind the desk and folded her hands.

Some time later the young guy came back, banging through the office door so suddenly that Adair jumped and Daniel woke from a seminap. "Okay, Mrs. Streiker," he said, placing a large radio on the desk and plugging it into the wall socket. "I'm gonna tune you in," he advised, turning a dial and taking up the microphone. "Ah, Blackbird, this is the Nest. Come in, Blackbird. Over."

Fletcher's voice responded, "Blackbird here. Got Mama and Baby Bird there? Over."

The radio guy showed her which button to depress to speak. "We're here," she said. *Over*, mouthed the radio guy, and she added, "Over."

"Good. You just listen in, and don't break in unless you have an emergency. We'll reach our destination in about a half hour. Over," Fletcher said.

"I understand. Over," she replied, then hooked the microphone back on the radio.

He flipped a switch on an intercom sitting on the desk. "You're all set there, Mrs. Streiker—I gotta get back to the airstrip now. Nobody should bother you here, so you just wait and listen to the radio for what's happening. Don't worry about a thing. Prince'll be here to take you home if something goes bust," he said reassuringly, and Adair looked at him bleakly. "Uh, yeah, well, laydahs," he said, leaving hurriedly.

Pensively, Adair sat down in front of the radio. Daniel lay down on the desk and spread his blankie over him. For a while they heard nothing, then somebody made a comment about the whitecaps below them. Daniel sat up, looking with renewed interest at the sound box.

"Okay, Blackbird, destination in sight," said one voice—Spud, she decided.

"Fall in easy. No mixing it up for fun, now; you make your purchase and get out," Fletcher reminded them.

A few more minutes of silence as Adair chewed her nails. "Go, Goose," Fletcher's voice said. That meant he had reached the house, she reasoned.

"Roger," Tommy responded.

Suddenly somebody exclaimed, "Firepower from the fields at six o'clock, Blackbird! Get up, get up!" There was some faint crackling.

"We're dropping our presents. Pelican, hit the fields," Fletcher said.

"Roger," Spud answered.

Adair was so intent on listening to the radio that she did not hear the back door of the room, the door to the alleyway, open. "Daniel," a feminine voice said.

Adair startled, and Daniel scampered down from the desk to rush to the one who had spoken. She was a willowy, beautiful woman with shimmering black hair like Daniel's. "You didn't tell anyone our secret, did you? You didn't say a word about it, now?" she asked Daniel lovingly, holding his chin. "Mommy missed you, baby. I've come to take you home. We're going to live far away where that bad man won't ever find us. You're going to get a new name, and live with

Mommy forever and ever."

"Who . . . you . . . ," Adair stammered.

"Comin' atcha from three o'clock! Get outta there, man! Go on!" shouted Spud over the radio.

"I see them," Fletcher said calmly. "Pelican—" His voice was suddenly obscured by loud static.

The woman looked up at Adair with frosty, cunning eyes. "No, I didn't die, but I was hurt badly enough to need a lot of plastic surgery. I just so happened to find a friend at the hospital who didn't care for Fletcher, either, and arranged a death certificate for me. The only problem was Daniel—Daniel knew, but you kept your promise not to tell, didn't you, baby?" She stroked his cheek adoringly and he gazed up at her.

The radio crackled fitfully. "Goose? Come in, Goose!" Fletcher demanded, sounding strained.

"They got him! They're coming! Give us thirty seconds!" Tommy's voice crackled over the radio.

"Blackbird, permission to fire!" came Spud's voice.

"Negative, Pelican," Fletcher said. Spud's reply was lost in static.

"How did you know we were here?" Adair asked helplessly.

"Fletcher has a lot of enemies, and one of them works here," she replied with a satisfied smirk.

*And in Paia, and Dallas, and Honolulu . . . ,* Adair thought, suddenly dizzy at the number of enemies surrounding them.

"Time to go, Daniel." Sandra took him by the hand and began leading him out.

Heavy crackling over the radio, and then silence. "Stop—wait—you mustn't do this," Adair pleaded.

"Take my son? You can count on it," she replied with a toss of her head. "There's no real reason Fletcher should want him, anyway."

*Not want his own son?* Adair thought in disbelief, feeling the desperate urge to tackle her and pound her head on the floor a few times. But as she watched Daniel holding on to the mother he had not seen for a year, she realized that it wouldn't do any good. As long as Daniel wanted to go with her, there was nothing Adair could do to stop them. Apparently realizing this, Sandra lingered in taking Daniel to inflict as much pain as possible on Adair.

Spitting and hissing, the radio came back on, and Sandra paused to listen. "Got him! We got him!" Tommy shouted.

"Then get out! We're right behind you. Pelican, you're right over the fields. See any booby traps?" Fletcher asked.

"Affirmative, Bossman," Spud replied.

"Can you set them off?" Fletcher asked.

"That's an affirmative," Spud said gleefully. Seconds later there were pops and whoops of laughter.

The woman reached out for the back door handle. "Daniel," Adair begged, and he looked back. "Daniel, you know he loves you," she whispered.

"Good job. Okay, anyone hurt?" Fletcher's voice asked.

"Negative, Boss," Tommy replied.

"How's Harle?" Fletcher asked.

"He's okay, Boss, just a little feverish. He keeps calling for someone. He keeps saying, 'Sandra, Sandra,'" Tommy answered.

There was a second of silence, then Fletcher demanded, "Mama Bird? Is everything all right there? Over."

"Go ahead and answer him," Sandra laughed. "Tell him all about it. By the time he gets here, it won't matter."

Ignoring her, Adair focused on Daniel. "We love you, Daniel. You know we do. Who tells the truth, Daniel? Which one of us tells the truth, your first mommy or me? You kept your promise, and you were good to do that, but your mommy lied, Daniel. She lied about your daddy and she lied about being dead. She lied to her own mommy and hurt her very much."

Daniel studied Adair, and a shadow crossed his face. "Daniel understands that I did what I had to do to protect him," Sandra said defensively.

"Adair? Is anything wrong? Over," Fletcher asked over the radio.

"If you go with her, she'll never let you see your daddy again," Adair warned Daniel. "If you want me to, I'll stop her—but only if you want me to."

"Daniel knows how much that man would hurt him if he ever got the chance," Sandra said confidently, pulling his arm. "Let's go now."

Adair stepped around the desk. "Who pulled you from the ditch?" she cried. Daniel looked bewildered.

"Adair! Answer me! Over!" Fletcher demanded.

"Daniel," Adair appealed with tears, "don't let her take you away from your daddy again. He loves you."

As Daniel stared up at Adair, something clicked in his eyes. He had gotten his first taste of fatherly love and discovered he liked it. Sandra had failed to recognize the hunger in all little boys for a father's attention. That hunger can be suppressed or denied as any appetite can, but given a choice, almost any boy would choose to fill it. Daniel looked at the alternatives of life with his father versus life without him and made his decision.

He made an about-face toward Adair, but Sandra jerked him back. "Prince, check the back room," Fletcher's voice said.

Adair pushed off from the desk and took Sandra's arm in a solid grip. "You try to take him when he doesn't want to go, and I'll break your face," Adair breathed.

Sandra stepped away as if backing down, then spun around to rake her fingernails across Adair's face, aiming for her eyes. Adair was quick enough to avoid much damage, but it startled her so that she lost her hold on Sandra's arm.

Breaking free, Sandra shoved Adair backward into the desk, scattering paperwork, and ran with Daniel toward the alleyway door. Adair jumped up and threw herself onto Sandra's back as she paused to open the door. They fell to the floor with a thud. Fletcher was demanding a response over the radio, but Adair did not hear him.

Daniel squirmed out from between them to scramble under the desk. At that moment the other door opened, and a native Hawaiian who looked to be carved out of several tons of stone lumbered in and regarded the two women wrestling on the floor. Sandra was yanking Adair's hair as Adair tried to pin her hands to the floor. He gravely considered the situation, then bent over and separated them. Holding Adair around the ribs with one arm, he picked up Sandra with the other.

Sandra twisted and bit him savagely on the arm. He quickly let go, and she darted out of the back door. Panting, Adair hung on his beefy arm, then blinked at the blood oozing from the teeth marks on his other arm. "She's mean!" Adair exclaimed, rubbing her head.

When Prince let her down she dropped to her hands and knees to look under the desk where Daniel hid. He reached out to her, and Adair dragged him out to sit on the floor and squeezed the stuffings out of him.

"Prince? Adair? I'm waiting very patiently for someone to answer. Over," Fletcher said in an ominous singsong.

Adair exhaled, then got up unsteadily to put Daniel on the desk beside the radio. She depressed the talk button and said as calmly as possible, "We're here. Um, Sandra showed up to try to take Daniel, but he didn't want to go. Over."

"Is he there? Is he there with you? Over," Fletcher asked quickly.

"Yes, he's here." Trembling slightly, she held the microphone up to Daniel's face. "Would you like to tell your daddy that you're all right?" she suggested.

Daniel concentrated on the microphone and opened his mouth, but a year's worth of silence was most difficult to break. Without speaking, he stuffed his blankie in his mouth and leaned against Adair. "He wanted to talk to you, but he just couldn't get it out," she said, sitting weakly. "Over."

"As long as he's all right. Over," Fletcher said.

"Yes. Is Harle okay? Over," she asked.

There was a brief pause, then Harle's voice said thinly, "I might be okay if people would quit jerking me around all over creation. Over."

"Gripe, gripe, gripe. Be a man, Harle, okay?" Adair returned testily and there was a burst of masculine laughter.

"Prince, why don't you cart those two to the hospital so she can encourage Harle in person? We'll be there in about an hour. Over," said Fletcher.

"Garans, Boss. Over," uttered Prince.

"Over and out, then," replied Fletcher.

❦

In an hour Adair was standing nearby as Harle was transferred from a gurney to a hospital bed. With his

231

neck, chest, and midriff swathed in bandages, he reached an upturned hand to Daniel. "Hey, man. Give me five." Daniel slapped his hand and Adair bent down to kiss Harle's cheek.

"You're fired," Fletcher said, entering in time to witness the kiss.

"Wait'll you get my last expense voucher. That'll knock some zeroes out of your account," Harle said gruffly.

"After getting the Blackbird all shot up again. You're a lot of trouble, Harle." Grinning, Fletcher grabbed his hand, then kissed Adair and picked up Daniel, who buried his face on his father's shoulder. Fletcher closed his eyes as he held him.

"Shot up? And no one got hurt?" Adair asked.

"Nah. When the Blackbird was repaired after you and I were fired on, I had it bulletproofed like the other two. It just looks like it's been in a hailstorm, now," Fletcher said, shaking his head over another repair bill.

"Then—they found Harle in the condo," Adair said, squeezing Harle's hand.

"I'll be pickin' glass outta my hair for a week, from when they broke the window," Harle groused as he felt his head.

"Found him in the condo," Fletcher said, nodding, "but the killdeer attracted enough attention for the others to get him out. I understand the Kona police received an anonymous tip about a marijuana crop and weapons cache at the estate. Wonder if that line of patrol cars we passed had anything to do with that."

Adair turned back to Harle. "And you knew about Sandra coming to try to take Daniel?"

"Yeah—heard them talking it all out. Bailey," Harle said, poking a finger at Fletcher. "Bailey at Ono is the one who told them when you left. But he wasn't in the back room and he didn't know you were going to hit the condos."

"Bailey," Fletcher repeated thoughtfully, nodding. "I'll take care of him."

"Now how was it that this big guy—Prince—heard you tell him to check on us?" Adair demanded.

"I had Prince listen through the intercom, but I told him to stay out unless he heard otherwise," Fletcher answered. "He's downstairs getting a tetanus booster for that bite."

"He'd better get a rabies shot, while he's at it," Harle growled.

"Oooooh," Adair said.

Fletcher regarded her, shaking his head. "That's one fight I'm sorry I missed. Throw in a little mud—I could've sold tickets and doubled my net worth." Harle laughed and then groaned, holding his bandages. Adair pretended to glare, but she was just too proud of herself to make it convincing. She stroked Daniel's head lovingly, pressed against her thigh.

A nurse suddenly entered and ordered, "All right, everybody out. We're going to change bandages and see what kind of damage you jokers have done."

Humbly, Fletcher yielded; but he paused to say, "Good to have you back, Harle."

"Thanks, Boss," Harle replied with a lazy grin.

They stepped out to leave him in the nurse's hands. Fletcher then told Adair, "Leo held me up on the way here to tell me that Desirée has been calling all over looking for me. She wants us to come over tomorrow to have dinner with them."

"Oh, Fletcher! That'd be great!" she said, hugging him.

"Yeah. She has a good heart," Fletcher admitted. A moment later he mused, "So Sandra finally showed. I

233

knew it was all too coincidental—all these connections to the Warfield Group."

"She made Daniel promise to not say a word about her being alive. He kept his promise, and then some," she said, touching the babyish cheek. "But you knew she was alive. How did you know?"

"I didn't trust the doctor from the very first—the one who was on duty when she was brought in after the accident. So I kept tabs on him, and when I learned of his new clinic I went back and did some checking on the accident. It didn't take much to uncover the fake autopsy. I knew she'd been watching you for an opportunity to take Daniel. When I heard about the Warfield Group today, I realized that she'd probably make her move while I was gone. I went ahead and left Daniel with you because he knows you better than me. If anyone could stop Sandra from taking him, it would be you," he said.

"Will you let her see him, if she asks to?" Adair wondered.

"She won't ask. She won't approach me directly—she'll just hang around for an opportunity to steal him again," he said.

"You think so? What are you going to do?" she gasped.

"*We're* going to watch over the nest until Daniel is big enough to fend her off for himself," Fletcher said.

She stammered, "But—her, and the Warfield Group—and that guy at Ono who tipped them off that we'd be there, and—the guy at the park in Dallas—"

"You're not getting paranoid, are you, Adair?" he asked, and she gazed at him with troubled eyes. "I know about them. I know about all of them. Trouble is, I can't just wipe everybody off the face of the earth who hates my guts. What I *can* do is cultivate friends all over—

like Brian and your parents—who will help me meet their sneak attacks. It's kind of like guerrilla warfare. Down and dirty. But I don't worry much, 'cause I've got a lot more resources than the Warfield Group does," he said.

Adair silently grappled with this, then asked, "You think you can use my parents after all?"

He shrugged. "They did everything I suggested, and that's a promising start. If they'd have insisted on hanging on to the things that were such problems for them, then we'd never get anywhere."

"I'd introduce you to my father, if I could find him," she mused.

"He's staying at a fleabag motel in Dallas," Fletcher answered, startling Adair. "We'll fly back and have a talk with him as soon as it's feasible. Meanwhile, I'm keeping tabs on him."

As they exited the hospital into the parking lot, he hefted Daniel high over his head. The child squealed happily and kicked his skinny legs. "And as for *you*, Mr. Daniel Travis Streiker, I'm gonna take *you* to the nearest toy store and buy you all the cars and trucks and laser blasters that we can fit into the car! And then we'll make another trip! We'll fill up your room with toys until there's no place to walk! And then I'm gonna buy you a closet full of cool shoes and a beach full of pretty pebbles! How 'bout that?" he demanded, shaking Daniel while the boy cackled until he was breathless.

"So," Fletcher lowered Daniel back to his shoulder and asked Adair, "what would you like to eat tonight?"

"Peesa!" cried Daniel.

"What?" gasped Fletcher, and Adair drew in a quick breath. "What did he say?" he demanded, turning to her.

"Peesa!" Daniel reiterated, curling his arms back over his head and grinning at his father's reaction.

"Pizza!" exclaimed Adair.

Daniel gazed in gratification at Fletcher, stricken speechless with joy. Then a grin spread across the father's face that was mirrored in the face of his son, and Fletcher declared, "This calls for a party to end all parties. Tonight!"

# 16

I f it weren't Honolulu's finest restaurant, it was one of the friendliest. Tonight, it was also one of the busiest. Every room and patio in the place was crowded with boisterous patrons. They should have been happy; it was all-you-can-eat, free. However, customers who showed up uninvited were apologetically turned away from the private party.

The volume of the conversation and laughter was so high that no one could hear the band trying to play. The musicians were plenty offended until the Man himself paid them in cash and invited them to help themselves from the buffet until a later hour, when the crowd would be more likely to settle down and listen.

Part of the problem was the children, who ran around like heathen from room to room and table to table, making an unearthly racket and generally having a splendid time. Since the Man merely smiled at their mayhem, no one else felt inclined to make the kids sit like adults and be bored to death. Any grown-up nearby merely hauled up any child who was running danger-ously, or brandishing a spit, or trying to throw a smaller child into the pool of Japanese carp.

"Daddy," whined the voice at Fletcher's elbow, and he turned. "He pushed me and I fell down and hurt myself," Daniel complained, pointing at the perpe-trator.

Not having realized Daniel to be the Man's son, the bigger boy blanched. "I didn't either! It was a accident!"

"You did too!" Daniel swung an angry fist at him.

"I did not!" the boy protested.

"Daddy, he pushed me!" Daniel maintained.

Fletcher glanced at Adair, seated on his right, and she flashed an inquiring smile at him. Turning back to Daniel, he suggested, "Why don't you sit on my lap, then, so you won't get hurt?"

"No!" Daniel scurried away, sneaking a swipe at the bigger boy as he passed.

Seated across the table from Fletcher, Aunt Margot sighed as she watched Daniel scoot away. "Your father was always getting into fights when he was that age. He wasn't ornery; he just felt called upon to challenge every bully around, no matter how much bigger they were. Our mother got so tired of mending his clothes that she finally assigned me to keep him out of trou-ble. Oh! What an impossible task!"

Those around her laughed because the exclamation was uttered in all seriousness. Desirée added, "Mother said that's why he joined the Navy—so he could take on trouble and get paid for it. I guess it runs in the family."

Fletcher arched a brow at her mischievous look. "And what are we implying?" he asked haughtily.

From nowhere Daniel appeared again at his father's

elbow. "Daddy," he whined, "they won't let me have any fish food to feed the fish. Make them give me some so I can feed them, too!"

Fletcher turned in bemusement to Adair. "Why were we so anxious to get him to talk?"

She shrugged, smiling. "So he'll come bug you for what he wants and I won't have to read his mind anymore?" she suggested.

"Oh," he said.

"Charity, go help Daniel get some food out of the dispenser," Desirée instructed.

"Okay, Mom." The eight-year-old obediently got up from her chair and took Daniel's hand, placing a guiding arm around his shoulders. "C'mon, Dan'l; I'll get it for you."

"Thank you, Charity," Adair said as they trotted off. "Looks like she inherited your job," she added to Margot.

"Excuse me?" said Margot, leaning forward. Adair repeated herself. "Oh, my. Good luck, dear," Margot called after the girl. "Anyway, as I was saying, the commotion at the church after you left the funeral was just something! But that preacher—*where* did you find him, Desirée?" Margot interrupted herself to ask.

"He called to volunteer after Pastor Cho got sick at the last minute. I assumed he was an associate," Desirée explained tiredly, as if for the hundredth time.

"Well, he never did get his steam back, let me tell you. We just had a hymn and prayer and closed. It was quite sufficient. Afterward, *everybody* was coming up to me and congratulating me as if *I* had done something. It was all quite amusing," Margot said, dipping her shrimp in sauce.

"I thought so," Fletcher admitted, glancing slyly at Desirée. She rolled her eyes and exhaled in resignation.

"Tell me," Adair wondered, shaking the ice in her

tea glass, "will you ever outgrow tormenting your sister?"

"I hope not," Fletcher replied in a scandalized tone.

Daniel reappeared beside Fletcher, whining, "Daddy—"

"What? What? What?" Fletcher roared, scooping him up and hanging him nearly upside down to tickle him. Daniel shrieked and kicked and laughed until he was breathless, then Fletcher sat him upright on his knee and said calmly, "Now what is it you wanted?"

Daniel had to pause while the laughs ran themselves down, then with a look of irritation he said, "I don't 'member."

"Then why don't you just sit still for a minute?" Fletcher suggested, covering the boy with his arms.

Charity came up, chagrined that Daniel had slipped past her. Desirée put a loving arm around her. "Adair," Desirée began hesitantly, "Panny was telling me earlier that you had turned down two dance companies to come out here. I'm wondering if you could find time to give Charity ballet lessons. She wants so badly to take, but we don't know who we could trust."

Hopeful and wide-eyed, Charity looked up at her aunt. "Do you want to?" Adair asked. Charity nodded vigorously. "I'd be delighted," Adair smiled. "We'll need a studio," she considered, then turned to Fletcher. "Is there one room in that nice big house that we could convert to a studio?"

"I bet we could find one," he smiled, regarding her.

Charity broke from her mother's side and began dancing in anticipation. Then they all looked out toward the beach upon hearing the sound of a conch-shell trumpet.

Charity darted around the table to seize Daniel by the hand. "C'mon, Daniel; they're lighting the torches! Let's go watch!" she cried. Daniel slid down from

STREIKER THE KILLDEER

Fletcher's lap and ran to watch from the patio railing.

As Fletcher looked after them, Spud came up with a Styrofoam carton. "We're taking some *huli huli* out to Harle, Boss."

"Good," Fletcher said, still watching his son across the room. "Tell him if he gets himself into any more trouble, I'm docking his next paycheck for the inconvenience of fishing him out."

"Oooh, bummahs," Spud noted seriously. "Laydahs."

"Bye, Spud," Adair said as he left.

Fletcher looked across the porch to the beach, where the men in *kapa malo* ran from torch to torch, lighting them. Blasts from the conch shells and beats from the drums accompanied them until, the task completed, they paddled across the dark water in their double-hulled canoes.

"I have something to tell you all," he said, and his companions looked at him expectantly.

"I am Daniel's father," he said deliberately, "but I'm not his *biological* father."

"What?" Adair said blankly, and the others stared.

"Sandra and I never slept together, you know my standards—her sometime boyfriend was Daniel's father. But when he was born, Sandra named me as father on the birth certificate, as leverage for his support. Word about that got back to me before she had even left the hospital. I went there to confront her about it—I knew it would be easy enough to prove that I was not responsible, with a blood test.

"But when I got there, and saw Daniel, I changed my mind. I decided that if I was named as his father on paper, then I would be his father in fact. I made him my son that day," Fletcher said.

"Why?" Adair blurted.

"I saw him and loved him. I chose him to be mine,

241

just like I chose you," he said with a faint smile.

Margot gaped at him, then broke into a wide smile. "Well done, Fletcher!" she whispered.

"But Fletcher—he even looks like you!" Adair insisted.

He grinned, "Sure he does. You were looking for a resemblance, so you found one."

Desirée exclaimed in accusation, "You told me he was yours!"

"When I told you that Sandra had a child, you jumped to the conclusion that I was the father," Fletcher corrected her. "I decided if that was what you were inclined to believe, I'd just let you think that for a while. Besides, I wanted you to accept Daniel as fully and completely mine, not just as an adopted child."

Flabbergasted, Desirée asked in a hurt voice, "Why . . . why did you think it would matter to me that he was adopted?"

Fletcher just eyed her till she looked away guiltily.

"Sandra told her own mother the baby was yours," Adair recalled.

Fletcher nodded, "Sure. She intended to squeeze as much as possible out of me, and used her mother to spread the story."

"What did Sandra do when you claimed him? You still tried to marry her," Adair said, half in question.

"Yes, to give Daniel legitimacy. She was quite surprised—it never crossed her mind that I would actually want him. I knew she wouldn't accept; she didn't want a relationship, just cash. So she took off with him. And I quietly pursued, because Daniel needed me," Fletcher related.

Adair was still raking her memory for clues. "You know, when Harle introduced me to Daniel, my first impression was that he was adopted. But Harle said he was yours."

"Harle had seen the birth certificate. He didn't know the rest," Fletcher replied.

"Why didn't you tell us sooner? Didn't it bother you that all the rest of your family thought you had fathered an illegitimate child?" Desirée asked, still stinging over his earlier comments.

"I told you as soon as I had you all together, as soon as the time was right," he shrugged. "I knew you'd learn the truth eventually. But rightly or wrongly, my name is on that birth certificate, and I wasn't going to abandon my own child."

"Whew—then anybody could get away with putting you down as father on a birth certificate," Clay said, breaking out into a sweat.

Fletcher smiled cagily. "And I'll take responsibility for it. But it also means the child is mine to raise."

Adair recalled what Fletcher had said about training her young stepbrother, Brian, and putting him to work. And she thought about the love and the foresight that would compel him to invest so much in undervalued lives.

Absorbing all this, they looked across the room at the children squealing over the light show. Adair wondered, "Does Daniel know how fortunate he is?"

"When he can understand, we'll tell him," Fletcher replied.

Desirée couldn't deal with any more of this at present, so she determinedly changed the subject: "So— when will your family be here, Adair?"

Adair shifted mental gears. "Ah, next week. Fletcher is flying them out to visit over the Thanksgiving holiday," she replied with slightly less enthusiasm. "Just for four days. He wants them to meet Daniel. He wants everybody to meet Daniel."

"He's a cute kid, even without the Streiker genes,"

Clay observed, stealing a glance at his wife before looking back over his shoulder. Daniel was trying to climb the patio railing and Charity was trying to keep him down.

"He's a handful," Adair said, placing her napkin on the table. "Excuse me." And she went over to help Charity restrain him from diving over the railing.

Desirée looked after Adair, then turned to remark quietly, "You chose a good mother for your son. You're very lucky, Panny."

He nodded thoughtfully. "I am very blessed." Then he rose from the table and walked over to the railing, where Adair held Daniel still to look at night over the ocean.

Fletcher came up behind her and placed his hands on her arms. Adair smiled over her shoulder at him; Daniel sleepily tilted his head back to regard his parents together. His little fingers twined in Adair's dress, searching for his blankie.

"Daniel needs a little sister to torment," Fletcher suggested softly in her ear.

"What if he gets a little brother instead?" she asked wryly.

"Then we'll just have to keep trying," he whispered, holding her.

Daniel twisted in her arms, burying his face contentedly in her dress, and closed his eyes. "I feel sorry for Sandra," she said quietly. Fletcher said nothing. "Did she honestly believe she was doing Daniel any good to separate him from you?"

Fletcher stirred, exhaling. "I think at first she acted out of fear. But then when she saw how easy it was to thwart me—that I wasn't going to come after her with an army—it became kind of a game. It gave her a feeling of power to deprive me of the one thing I wanted most from her. At that point, I don't believe she gave a second thought to what was good for Daniel. Her first and foremost concern was herself."

"A little brown bird is a better parent than she was," Adair observed tightly.

"Sandra has gotten just what she earned for her performance as a mother," he noted, and she glanced up inquiringly. "She's been fired," he said.

"And you, lady," he whispered, leaning down on the railing to look up in her face, "whatever you want, for the rest of your life, is yours."

"Daniel!" Charity came running up, and he blinked and sat up. "Come on, Daniel; they're serving dessert!"

He clambered down from Adair's arms as she looked over to their table. "I want some *haupia*," she said.

Grinning, Fletcher straightened off the railing. "Come and get it."

⌒

*When they had finished eating, Jesus said to Simon Peter,*
*"Simon son of John,*
*do you truly love me more than these?"*
*"Yes, Lord," he said, "you know that I love you."*
*Jesus said, "Feed my lambs."*
JOHN 21:15, NIV

245

# Glossary

*aloha* (ah LO ha)—hello; love

*aole* (ah OH lay)—no

**brah** (bra)—brother; friend

**bummahs**—bummer; bum deal

**cockaroach**—to steal small items

**da kine** (da kyne)—all-purpose word meaning whatever the speaker chooses

**dah makule guys** (da mah KUH lay guys)—senior citizens

**garans**—guaranteed

*haole* (HOW lee)—Caucasian

*hapa* (HAH pa)—half

*haupia* (how PEE ah)—coconut custard

*hele mai ai* (HEY lay MY EYE)—come and eat

*huli huli* (HU lee HU lee)—barbecue

*kalua* (ka LU ah)—meat, most often pork, roasted in a pit oven

*kane* (KAH nay)—man

*kapa* (KAH pah)—tapa cloth made from bark of the mulberry tree and brightly painted *keiki* (KAY key)—child

*lau lau*—meat and potatoes wrapped in leaves and steamed

laydahs—later

*lolo* (low low)—stupid

*lomi* (LOW me)—massage; raw salmon "massaged" with spices

*mahalo nui loa* (mah HAH low NEW ee LOW ah)—thank you very much

*malihini* (ma la HEE nee)—stranger; tourist

*malo* (MAH low)—traditional loincloth worn by men

*nani* (NAH nee)—beautiful

*ono* (OH no)—delicious

*opihi* (oh PEE hee)—ocean limpets served raw, a delicacy

Panny (PAH nee)—short for *paniolo* (pa nee O lo), "cowboy"

*pau* (pow)—finished

*pehea oe* (pay HAY ah OY)—how are you?

*pilikia* (pee lee KEE ah)—trouble

*poi* (poy)—staple dish made from the taro root

*pupule* (pu PU lay)—crazy

*shaka* (SHAH kah)—great; perfect

swell head—angry

*wahine* (wah HEE nay)—woman

*wikiwiki* (WE key WE key)—hurry

Other Books by Robin Hardy:

*The Chataine's Guardian*
*Stone of Help*
*High Lord of Lystra*
*Streiker's Bride*

Drug runners in Big Bend, Texas . . . ?
Watch for a new novel by Robin Hardy
coming in 1994.